YOUR PLACE OR MINE?

YOUR PLACE OR MINE?

Practical Advice for Developing a
Co-Parenting Arrangement After Separation

CHARLOTTE SCHWARTZ

DUNDURN
PRESS

Publisher and acquiring editor: Kwame Scott Fraser | Editor: Robyn So
Cover designer: Laura Boyle

Library and Archives Canada Cataloguing in Publication

Title: Your place or mine? : practical advice for developing a co-parenting arrangement after
   separation / Charlotte Schwartz.
Names: Schwartz, Charlotte (Family law clerk), author.
Description: Includes index.
Identifiers: Canadiana (print) 20220233152 | Canadiana (ebook) 20220233209 | ISBN
   9781459750050 (softcover) | ISBN 9781459750067 (PDF) | ISBN 9781459750074 (EPUB)
Subjects: LCSH: Joint custody of children—Canada. | LCSH: Separated parents—Canada.
Classification: LCC KE600 .S33 2022 | LCC KF547 .S33 2022 kfmod | DDC
   346.7101/73—dc23

We acknowledge the support of the Canada Council for the Arts and the Ontario Arts Council for our publishing program. We also acknowledge the financial support of the Government of Ontario, through the Ontario Book Publishing Tax Credit and Ontario Creates, and the Government of Canada.

Dundurn Press
1382 Queen Street East
Toronto, Ontario, Canada M4L 1C9
dundurn.com, @dundurnpress 𝕏 f ⓞ

For the four of you kids, and the two of you dads.

We know today that our bodies keep a complete and faultless record of all the things we have ever experienced.

■

Back then … I would fall for almost anything … I thought that, like Lucy and Ricky Ricardo, my parents' fights just meant they loved each other in a noisy way.

Wally Lamb, *She's Come Undone*

Contents

Introduction

THE FIRST TIME I WROTE THIS INTRODUCTION WAS IN THE PANDEMIC newlywed stage. We all just needed to come together, do our parts, hunker down, and endure "two weeks to flatten the curve." I was scared of the unknown but hopeful that it would be over soon, and that later we could laugh about how we had overreacted during that first visit to Costco and binge-watched end-times-themed movies on Netflix to pass the boring time at home.

Then, in just a couple of days, my world went from one that thrived on structure to one that failed to provide it at every turn. I had to start working exclusively from home (in the BC — before coronavirus — era, going to my office had been an escape); the kids' schools were shuttered indefinitely; our child-care provider could no longer work, in the name of physical distancing; and I had to figure out how to work efficiently, care for our home, care for four kids, and care for myself, all at once. None of the things we ended up choosing during that time felt like choices, because none of them felt voluntary. Just the lesser of the evils available to us.

The pandemic could have also meant an about-face for my already co-operative relationship with Steve, the father of my two boys. We were both fortunate to remain employed in this unanticipated climate, and that's where the trouble could reasonably have begun. When it became apparent that we were about to be at home for a really long time, we were almost immediately thrust back into the familiar positions we had found ourselves in during our marriage when one of our kids was sick: *Whose job is more important today? If someone loses their job because of this, whose job is the easier one to lose? If someone needs to work and care for the sick kid, who can do that with more ease?*

Steve and I agreed right away that the boys' residential schedule (where they spend their nights, after-school hours, and weekends) would not change. Then the courts in Ontario did the same thing, telling inquiring parents that they "ought not to" change the residential schedules set for their children simply because of the pandemic. The courts took it a step further and said such upheaval would have a greater negative impact on the children than would the world's state of affairs. In their view, there was no good reason to dismantle the little structure that did remain for the kids by creating even more change, unnecessarily.

Of course, there were families that felt they had no choice but to change their schedules because one parent was a front-line medical professional, police officer, paramedic, or grocery store worker, and at that time there was no vaccine on the horizon, and we had very little information about the disease.

In our case, what had to change were the kids' days. Without school, they had five hours and fifty-five minutes of unclaimed daytime during which they suddenly needed to be cared for. Despite priding ourselves on comprehensive, watertight agreements (by family law standards), what no separation agreement or parenting plan in the history of humankind has ever foreseen is an unexpected and indefinite period of school and daycare closures in response to a global pandemic.

Oh no, they have not.

And then the courts did something they'd never done before: they mostly closed their doors.

Whereas, in the before-times, you could run to court on almost no notice to attempt to address issues that you thought were urgent, the courts began to triage matters that came in under the label *emergency*, determining who could and couldn't speak to a judge based on the severity of their circumstances.

People (myself included) were shocked to learn what constituted an emergency under these new temporary rules, and those who did not meet the urgency test were very much left to their own devices. Without saying it out loud, the court was doing something refreshing: they were looking people in the eye and telling them, "Resolve this, or wait." And the wait was indefinite. If you chose to wait, you were choosing many unknowns.

Without plans for the unplannable, countless families scrambled to make everything work, with very little guidance and with courts that intermittently closed their doors. Some, like Steve and me, can co-operate, but some absolutely cannot, for a myriad of reasons. For a lot of people, the closure of the court felt like calling 911 in an emergency and getting a busy signal.

It will be years before we can truly determine the way Covid-19 has changed the landscape, but one thing is certain: it has been a slap in the face. It has given us pause to examine our own actions. For Steve and me, it has been a time to come together and parent the hell out of a situation that has forever changed our kids' lives. That last part — the impact on children, not all of which we know yet — is by far the scariest.

When our skin has healed from all the handwashing and school has resumed consistently and there is a "new normal," I hope my children take from this experience that their dad and I made lemonade from these lemons. When we talk about Covid-19, I hope the children talk about the many life skills they learned with me and how much math and science they learned with their dad. I hope they'll make fun of my terrible French accent when I tried desperately to keep them learning, and that they'll fondly recall their dad's impeccable Spanish enunciation. I hope they remember parents who were undoubtedly stressed out but made the best of the worst.

It's the children of separated families whose parents cannot co-operate, those who were left by the roadside with a flat and no jack, that I worry about.

When I started my career in 2003, change was palpable in the family law world. Each year it seemed that those practising family law gained a better understanding of how damaging legal proceedings and messy divorces are to the most vulnerable participants entangled in them: the kids.

I hope this book brings you comfort if, as you embark on a separation or a divorce, you are staring down the road of co-parenting for many years to come and asking, "Will my kids be okay?" I hope that I make you laugh (mostly at my misfortune). And I hope you find my experiences relatable. I've made a lot of mistakes, and you probably will, too. I'll probably keep making them, trying to learn what I can along the way. The boxes at the end of each chapter highlight more of my personal experiences, but a few of them are about the experiences of those I interviewed.

For this book, I interviewed some people who were poorly parented or who (now regrettably) handled their own co-parenting relationships poorly. From reading their real accounts, I hope you learn how higher-conflict separation and divorce (or even higher-conflict circumstances in the home, without the added layer of a separation or divorce) can harm children in various stages of their development. I hope you understand that these hard facts about how children suffer could just as easily apply to you and your family. No one is immune. I hope you know that the outcome is in your hands.

And I hope you realize you can't do it all on your own and that help is out there.

Oren Lyons, a Chief of the Onondaga Nation, writes, "We are looking ahead, as is one of the first mandates given to us as chiefs, to make sure and to make every decision that we make relate to the welfare and well-being of the seventh generation to come.... What about that seventh generation? Where are you taking them? What will they have?" This ancient Haudenosaunee Seventh Generation Principle asks us to consider whether the decisions we make now will result in a sustainable world seven generations into the future. It may seem idealistic; our world is literally on fire and dealing with a pandemic. Still, the notion that we can make things better in the future — that we, individually, have the power to do that — is one of strength. I can choose to do everything in my power to improve things today, with the hope that tomorrow will be a little less bleak. That's all any of us can do collectively.

A former boss of mine used to ask clients in their initial consultations, "What is the worst thing that your ex would say about you?" The goal of this book is for your ex's answer to have nothing to do with the way you parent post-separation. Let their answer be about something that matters a lot less.

It was about six months into my newly separated life. My youngest son was in senior kindergarten, and when the weather abruptly turned from fall to winter, the way it always seems to in Toronto, I sent him to school layered up in a hoodie from his winter clothes stash. Like so many other little kids who complain about sleeves and cuffs and collars and textures and tags and scratchy things, my son complained to his teacher that his sleeve was itchy.

Not both sleeves, just one.

The teacher kindly unzipped his hoodie, mostly to appease him. She was probably going to mime the removal of the culprit non-thing, like a magician pulling metres of coloured fabric out of their nostril. Instead, she peeled from the static-cling force field of his sleeve's cheap polar fleece lining one of my nicest, fanciest pairs of underwear.

She was surprised, of course, and my son laughed his head off the way only a little kid would at the sight of a forty-eight-dollar red thong in a kindergarten classroom.

And then the teacher did what anyone would do: she pulled on a pair of latex gloves with a surgical *snap* and placed the underwear in a Ziploc bag. She added a handwritten note that read "I think these are yours." With a little smiley face.

Although they'd come from my house that morning, the boys were due to be at their dad's that night. So the *CSI* crime-scene evidence bag made its way there, unbeknownst to me, inside the backpack of my five-year-old son, who had already forgotten about it. Once the boys were in bed, their dad, as was his routine, unzipped their backpacks, removed half-eaten lunches, and looked for permission forms and the dirt and rocks and sticks that came home every day. And then he found the Ziploc bag.

He snapped a photo and sent it to me with a text: "I think these are yours?" And a shrugging-man emoji.

This was the first (and maybe the most embarrassing) of many times when I would realize that it would always be much easier not to hate each other.

Real life, I thought, *knows no fucking boundaries, does it?*

1

Between the End and the Beginning: Fear, Grief, and Higher Ground

SO YOU DID IT — YOU SEPARATED.

I know that it probably came after months, maybe even years, of contemplation, during which you were utterly worn down by the stresses of the unknown: *Is this right for the kids? Are we doing the right thing? Will the kids be okay? Have we tried everything? Can we afford it? Is this even what I want? What if I change my mind?*

Of course, there are all sorts of other questions and issues to sift through when a relationship comes to an end.

There are the boring things: the bank accounts to close and the house to sell and the pensions to divide. Those things are significant, but they are dealt with in a formulaic and predictable way. Each province and territory uses a mathematical equation. In Ontario, it's called *net family property*, which, in the most clinical and calculated way, takes everything you've worked for, compares it to everything your spouse has worked for, and draws a hard line down the centre. The difference between what each of you has is divided and then is said to have been "equalized." That's oversimplifying quite a bit, but this book isn't about property division.

And then there are the small things that are meaningful to you but of almost zero importance to lawyers and courts. Christmas decorations to divide into two neat piles — but who gets the "Baby's First Christmas" tree ornament? Sets of dishes to divvy up — but who will end up short one dinner plate because of that time the kids dropped a plate in the backyard after you'd begged them to use a paper one? And pieces of furniture to be distributed — they could be replaced, but those wouldn't have the memories we feel forever attached to. These things take up considerable time and headspace for most people. Realizing that, in the end, you're left with a pile of stuff worth whatever it would fetch at a yard sale is a tough, but necessary, rite of passage on your way to healing.

And then there is the other "thing": What happens with the kids?

With two loving, willing parents now living in separate homes several kilometres apart, where will the kids live? And when? How? Will anything ever feel normal again?

To contemplate not seeing your children every day — even their worst, neediest, most complaint-filled days — is heartbreaking. To think there will be nights when they won't be sleeping under your roof and, for maybe the first time, you won't tiptoe to their door to listen for the familiar timbre of their breathing is ... Well, it's the stuff family law nightmares are built on.

That initial heartbreak, though, quickly turns to anger and resentment. I'm sure these are part of the stages of grief we learn about in life. You may wonder why I refer to grief here. To be clear, no one has died. But a significant relationship has ended, and the same processes apply. When coming to terms with the end of one relationship and the start of another, grief is important, even though it is hard. The grief I experienced at the end of my marriage was so significant that it felt like a death, and I mourned it like one. I would be remiss if I didn't tell you that I still do sometimes.

I know that you tried everything, because I did, too. I know it has kept you up many nights. I know your stomach flip-flops when you think about it. I know how insecure you feel about all the question marks in your future.

I should have known that those feelings would be coming when I separated, because over the past twenty years, I have had the humbling and life-changing experience of sitting across the table from hundreds of people in various stages of separation or divorce. I'm a senior family law clerk. That's a terrible, vague title for a career that doesn't entail anything clerical. I meet with people one on one to cull the most personal of personal details, which will be woven together into their family law stories that a mediator or judge will, maybe, read one day. I work with talented senior family law lawyers to prepare clients for each step of their family law matter, whether it's going the traditional "kitchen table" route of negotiation with the aid of experienced lawyers, or to a mediator, or to court. I have a front-row seat to the drama — and trauma — that comes with the territory.

I have literally held the hands of folks as they navigate situations that feel impossible. I've given and received the kind of hugs you understand only if you've been through it. I've talked people off proverbial ledges. I've fought with people about doing simple things to avoid legal catastrophe (like convincing a well-to-do client to set his home up with internet access, in 2016, so his teenage children would continue to go to his house, in order to forgo a extremely costly motion). I have hugged people in tears, choking back my own. I have seen things go very badly in court, and I have marvelled, time and again, at how we would rather have a complete stranger make major decisions about our own families than make them ourselves.

I have also seen things go very well. What that actually means is that neither parent was happy, but the framework for happy children had been established. And twice I have worked on files where the couples, already knee-deep in separation, successfully reconciled.

Over the years, I have found the most fulfillment helping people arrive at a solid Plan B when their Plan A didn't work out. I gained intimate knowledge of what it feels like to have your life turned upside down, to have everything feel raw and exposed and uncertain, to have every issue arising from the breakdown of a relationship — parenting, support, property — staring you in the face, like some kind of family law Cerberus. A note here about language: Many families would not consider their parenting circumstances Plan B — for better or for worse. I refer solely to those families who did intend to parent as a couple, together in the same home, and not to the great many families who choose solo parenting, or who are solo parenting but did not make that choice actively, or who have multiple parents in the picture by choice.

I didn't know anything about family law before I became a law clerk. In fact, I didn't even know what a law clerk was or what one did. I wanted to be an actress and a comedy writer for *Saturday Night Live* and to change lives with my wit.

When my college-bound boyfriend asked me to move in with him, my parents made it very clear: at eighteen, I could move out, but I had to be in school, and I had to pay all my own expenses, including tuition. I went to my boyfriend's college; picked up a copy of the course book; and actually — for real — placed one hand over my eyes, flipped the pages of the book with the other, placed my index finger on a page, and then uncovered my eyes to see what I'd landed on. My three-inch acrylic nail was very clearly straddling the line between *Early Childhood Educator* and *Law Clerk Diploma Program*. So I applied to both, for a January intake, and chose the law clerk program after watching *Erin Brockovich*. I finished in just sixteen months and got the first job I applied for, at a boutique family law firm where I then spent the first five years of my career.

I got married and went on to have two little boys. I enjoyed eight years of marriage with a solid human who inspired me and who provided the conditions and sense of safety under which I *wanted* to grow up and to be better. I had not known that feeling before — that shelter of safety that people talk about. And I basked in it.

We did all the things in the right order: bought a house, got engaged, got married, had kids, renovated and took on the requisite second-mortgage debt. I worked hard during each of those stages, driven by an ever-increasing, and anxiety-inducing, desire to progress at everything. And I like to think I gave those years every single thing I had. We took carefully planned family road trips, made vague but promising plans for retirement on Canada's East Coast, and talked about flying somewhere for our tenth wedding anniversary. We were just like everyone else.

But somewhere along the way — I've learned you can never pinpoint the exact moment when the first invisible fracture is sustained — things fell apart. We ended up as part of a statistic I was already intimate with: the approximately 40 percent of people who, according to Statistics Canada in 2008, had two young kids, "irreconcilable differences," a lifetime ahead of us, and a marriage ending in divorce. This statistic does not account for families in which the spouses are unmarried (that is, common law) or that never took steps to formalize their separation or divorce. Still, it is widely accepted that around 40 percent (what people mean when they say "half") of legal marriages in Canada (skewing higher in more densely populated provinces) end in divorce, with that rate increasing year over year since 2001.

In the early days following my separation from Steve, I found it therapeutic to write. I even eulogized our marriage; I talked about the stages of grief even though no one had died, because they absolutely apply to these situations, too, and about the shock that lingered for a long time — too long — in our co-parenting relationship.

In our initial, anger-filled conversations, I — even with my significant experience in family law — uttered things to him like "Don't you dare think you're getting my kids half the time," along with a string of expletives that I'm not proud of. Each time, I had to stand back from what I'd just said and calm down. Of course the kids would be with their dad half the time. He is a great dad. I am a good mom. We are very different people, with very valuable things to contribute to our kids' lives. Nothing else would be the same, for sure, but the one constant would be our commitment to taking the best care of our kids.

Of course, *of course,* we would share them and play equal roles in their lives. It was what we had intended to do, what I had envisioned when I said in my wedding vows that I would dance with him that night and on our twenty-fifth anniversary. The steps were just going to look very different.

In the end, Steve and I conceived and raised a third child — a forty-eight-page separation agreement addressing as many hows and whens as we could anticipate. A structurally sound foundation for the rest of our lives, flanking our two boys, waving a white flag to life going on.

■

People ask how we did it at the time, and people ask how we still do it.

It's really, really (really!) hard to be friends (or friendly, even) with an ex-partner. Maybe the hardest thing. When children are involved, there's never that coveted clean break because, like it or not, you are forever connected. You are tethered by dates on a calendar and milestones to celebrate and hardships to weather together, as a family. Accepting that fact first, I think, plays a massive role in moving forward.

Perhaps it also helps that both of us are children of divorce and have seen things play out in our lives that we would never want for our own kids. Perhaps it benefitted us that I have professional experience. I know, therefore, that only 1 percent of family law matters go to trial (the kind of court appearances sensationalized on TV and in movies like *Kramer vs. Kramer*) and that going to court — or, worse, to trial — costs approximately a gazillion dollars, which means that even if (and that's a big *if*) someone "wins," nobody truly does in the end.

Everything we do, good or bad, has a significant impact on our children's lives — forever. Life is short and childhood even shorter. With every opportunity to nurture these little humans, why would we choose anything but the best for them? Steve and I quickly decided that the kids would spend equal time in each of our homes, getting the best we could give them in this new regimen, this new businesslike partnership of parenting. The literature on this subject widely accepts that children deserve to have equal time and strong, loving, supportive relationships with each parent and that each parent should be supported and lifted up by the other parent, except for in certain and limited circumstances, where it is reasonable to assume the child may not be safe in the other parent's care, for a number of reasons.

Despite stories we may hear that only one partner is at fault in a separation, Dr. Jean Clinton, a child psychiatrist, author, and speaker at McMaster University, says that two-thirds of high-conflict separations are *bilateral*, meaning both parents are at war with each other. Before you determine that you're not at fault, find yourself a good, insightful friend — not one who will say whatever you want to hear, but one who will tell you whether you are a problem or not. If you are part of the problem, then you need to be part of the solution, too.

Dr. Clinton reminds us that one-third of cases are, sadly and most unfortunately, unilateral; one parent *is* the problem. In this tough situation, we need to focus on supporting the more reasonable parent. The reality is that both parents will still assert influence over their kids' lives. Finding a way to work with the less reasonable parent is the only way out, and support is crucial. A mental health practitioner who can support one or both parents will provide a lifeboat, and the more reasonable parent should do everything they can to get the other parent on board.

I interviewed dozens of folks for this book and among the co-parent cohort (past and present), the most common message I heard was that in order for you to become good co-parents, your relationship has to evolve. It has to become like a business partnership where, together, you manage the project of raising good kids.

I did not have a tremendous amount of support through my separation. In hindsight, I wish I had done more to surround myself with the types of supports I needed (more on that later), but I didn't. I didn't want to talk about my separation or to expose it right away in a professional context. Instead, I focused on making all the necessary arrangements with Steve to bring everything to a nice, neat close. In my case, it helped that we had primary goals about the kids to focus on, knowing their well-being was the most important thing.

Steve and I had many conversations and email exchanges to create the plans that would eventually become the big, important document governing our lives going forward. Some of those conversations were really tough. I found myself sad and regretful, questioning my choices, and worrying about our kids. During telephone calls to discuss our plans for the kids, I would stray onto other topics, as though we were still Steve and Charlotte, the married couple, and not whoever we were now. When Steve purposefully redirected things (which, admittedly, was absolutely necessary), it stung. I'll be honest: I'd get angry and end the conversation. Sometimes I'd follow up with an accusatory text that would go unanswered. I deemed his lack of engagement dismissive, but it actually came out of the utmost respect for both of us. I failed to recognize that this process was hard for him, too.

Eventually the conversations started to get easier. We were able to lightheartedly discuss what the boys had done that night or that morning while also making big and little plans for their futures. Anytime I teetered on the edge of getting upset about some small thing, such as not seeing my kids for a certain holiday or not waking up with them on their birthday or their first day of school, I used tools I had subconsciously created to get myself through those moments without getting upset or yelling or doing some other thing I'd regret.

Some people use mantras, deep breathing exercises, or the close-your-eyes-and-count-to-ten method. I use my memories. I remind myself that the likely reason behind my emotional reactions is that I will actually always love this person I'm co-parenting with. I needed to manage my feelings — the kind you sometimes feel you have little control over, the kind that send you into mama-bear territory.

I started to recall memories of the earlier part of our relationship, like this one: When Steve and I had been dating for only a couple of months, he invited me to attend a wedding with him. He was in the wedding party, which meant I'd be sitting at a table with strangers while he partied at the head table. I was young, outgoing, and friendly, and I liked to drink, so I knew I'd be okay. I agreed to go with him on the condition that he help me choose a dress. At the time, my wardrobe was mostly a collection of twenty-dollar club dresses, and I felt that the wedding of his private-school friends warranted something much nicer.

We went to the Queen Street Hudson's Bay store in Toronto and made our way to the massive dress section, where I managed to find a simple but elegant black dress. When we'd agreed it was "the one," I said I needed a purse to match. This ensemble didn't have the stuff-your-flip-phone-under-your-bra-strap vibe that I was used to. So we headed to the handbag section a floor below.

It was a summer Saturday afternoon and we were in a huge, bustling department store in downtown Toronto, all the conditions Steve doesn't like: malls, fashion, trends, shopping, crowds. I perused the purses, feeling their textures and examining their insides for zippered pockets or loud-coloured lining.

On the way to the purse section, I'd educated Steve on various styles of handbags, and I'd reduced it to math: dimensions and price point. So he knew what I was looking for. We were about twenty feet apart when Steve hoisted a handbag high above the display rack and exclaimed, "Charlotte! Here's a nice snatch!"

I looked at him with equal parts horror and adoration. He had only just learned that type of purse was called a clutch and had, understandably, used the wrong word. Still, the dozen or so handbag buyers in our immediate vicinity looked up, startled. *What is this man?* they must have thought. *And why did he just say "snatch" so loudly?*

As soon as he realized what he had said, he crumpled, the human form of the word *crestfallen*. With everyone's eyes on us, I whispered, "Clutch. He meant to say 'clutch.'" We quickly vacated the area and took the winning clutch to a checkout counter far away. We rarely shopped together after that.

That moment lasted about forty-five seconds, but in my mind, and in my heart, it remains one of the most endearing, honest, vulnerable moments I have witnessed. A reminder we are still just those people, too.

And so, with a bank of memories like that, I will always love this person — this *snatch*-yelling, poorly-versed-in-fashion person with whom I now share two kids. That love has evolved. It is no longer the exciting, romantic, spontaneous young-couple love we experienced in our early days, but it is, arguably, what is meant by *real love*, love rooted in mutual respect, admiration, support, and common objectives like raising great kids.

I remind myself of that moment, and of many others like it, when I feel I'm on the verge of boiling over, and it stops me in my tracks sometimes. I've learned that you put your effort into the relationships that do work, not into the ones that don't. I've also learned that you can have a relationship that works and one that doesn't with the very same person.

Aside from managing my feelings, I've employed a lot of other unscientific techniques to help me as I bump along in this co-parenting life. I say "bump along" because when it comes to the unexpected, all parenting — co-parenting, solo, or otherwise — even the smoothest of freshly paved roads, is inherently bumpy. Indeed, parenting is the bumpiest and most ever-evolving, turning-on-a-dime part of my entire life.

From a completely non-professional perspective, I am happy to share my other strategies, too.

Think of the End of Your Relationship in a Different Way

I have found that reframing the language you use about the end of your relationship or marriage (even if it was definitely someone else's "fault," even if they had the weirdest relationship with their mom, even if they wanted every drawer in the house Marie Kondo'd and you hated it, even if they spent too much money on mail-order collectible figurines) is extremely helpful. Viewing your relationship as a failure is a barrier to moving into new phases. Although I'm not a "live, laugh, love" person, I do find it effective to view our relationship as an accomplishment. Even when the living-together part is over. How many other things can you say you did every day for years? Probably not many.

And then, when you can acknowledge your relationship as an accomplishment, ask yourself what you learned from the experience and what you will do differently in your next relationship.

Recall the "Snatch" Moments

I find it helpful to remind myself of the funny or happy moments, like Steve yelling "snatch." Do this often. The memories will make you smile; they will turn things around.

Remember That You Are in Control

If you incite, or engage in, a high level of conflict, someone else, like a judge, will inevitably have to take control. You don't want that. I promise you that some random judge on some random day doesn't know you or your kids or your kids' needs. They don't care who watched too much sports and who scrolled on their phone too much, and they don't care who was responsible for the time your four-year-old had to go to the emergency room after swallowing a wing nut.

Remind yourself often that you and your co-parent are in control. It is best for everyone if you, together, are the ones to make major, life-altering decisions for your family. It is important to be flexible. Remember that in your married/partnered life, there were many by-the-minute decisions to make and you made them, somehow. That doesn't need to change now. Part of your new business partnership involves being joint architects of parallel lives. It is completely possible, even when it feels like it isn't.

Time *Will* Fly

Remember the adage that new parents are told when they're exhausted and rocking huge under-eye circles: the days are long, but the years are short. In my opinion, this applies to separated, co-parenting life way more than it does to parenting babies. Natalie, a midthirties entrepreneur and co-parenting mother of one, became incredibly attached to the idea of having her daughter in her care for nine overnights out of every fourteen. She was willing to spend thousands of dollars to argue for it, even with the risk of not succeeding. Interestingly, it was Natalie's mother who said, "Time moves so quickly and this won't matter in a few years." Natalie admits that her mother's observation was so on point that it was pivotal for her: What *was* she even fighting about? Thereafter she frequently reminded herself of that conversation and is now continually surprised at how quickly the time has passed since her separation from her daughter's father.

Treat Your Co-Parent as You Want to Be Treated

Many co-parents I interviewed expressed the importance of fighting for the co-parenting relationship you *want,* not for the one you have, if you want the relationship to be better.

Act toward your co-parent in the same manner you hope to be treated. Never, ever give up if you're sharing children with a person who is proving to be a bit difficult (or, if you prefer, less reasonable) — maybe because they're hurt or grieving or angry. (This does not refer to the very small percentage of parents who flat-out refuse to co-operate and prefer to run to court with every grievance or to parents who may be enduring their own mental health crises.)

Natalie puts it best: it's having patience when you have none left and having empathy for someone you'd maybe rather not empathize with. It's remembering that we model everything our children will learn about relationships as early as they can remember things. When your children recall memories of their parents, how do you want them to remember you?

So now it's time to get started. Ask yourself: What is the worst thing your ex would say about you?

"Never marry a man you don't want to be divorced from."

Arlene, a parent I interviewed as part of my research for this book, brought my attention to this excellent quote from the late Nora Ephron's book *I Feel Bad About My Neck*. Ephron, like me, was married and divorced and married and divorced and married again.

Arlene has a very healthy, open parenting dynamic. She and her ex-husband share their sixteen-year-old daughter between their two homes, and it is really all their daughter knows; she was six when they split up.

Arlene's ex-husband has since remarried and has gone on to have another child — a five-year-old girl, a half-sister to his daughter with Arlene. When a Covid-19 outbreak caused the five-year-old's school to close for two weeks, her teacher-mother panicked. Where would the girl go every day when both parents had to work outside of their home?

"Send her here," Arlene said. "I'm home anyway."

And home she was. In more ways than one.

2

Getting to the End: Your Support Network and First Steps

WHAT IS THE WORST THING YOUR EX WOULD SAY ABOUT YOU?

I had a client respond, "I broke up with her, after a twenty-five-year marriage, by sending a text message. Among other things, I communicated how much it bothered me that she didn't get along with my mother and sister. And then I blocked her number so I wouldn't have to see her response."

I imagine that partner in the moments after receiving that message, and I wonder what support system they had.

A separating family actually has a number of options, and the most solution-oriented are consistently promoted by lawyers. It's what I love about family law across Canada. What I hate about family law is that nearly all the "family law people" I know take their work home with them. I worry about clients, their kids, and their futures. I've gotten better at compartmentalizing, but I often find myself worrying. It's part of what makes me good at my job.

Family law is centred around creative resolutions and family-focused solutions to all the problems that could reasonably arise when the life of a family is flipped on its head. Most responsible family law practitioners (and I have had the pleasure of working alongside many) try to steer matters away from court. I believe that most people can achieve resolutions with strong support and a great team surrounding them. I also believe that most parents truly don't want to mess up their kids. But adults carry with them all forms of trauma, including unhealed and unresolved experiences from their childhoods, and they're doing the best they can reasonably do. If you're reading this book, you are doing just that. I know it can feel impossible to break generational cycles while parenting at the same time. It's work, every single day.

I'll add that intimidating statements like *I'll see you in court* or, my favourite, *Lawyer up!* are ridiculous, made-for-TV lines that no one should take seriously. Yet in anger-fuelled moments we let the words slip out without understanding that to the other person they feel like a declaration of war and an assault on their future.

Setting yourself up for success is key. And I in no way mean "winning"; I mean coming out of the process supported, healthy, and at least partially ready for the next steps.

Before we dive in, a note on the phrase *getting a divorce*. That language is limiting, and a lot of people don't understand the nuances, so I'll make it clear here. A divorce does not refer to dividing property, dealing with finances, or making parenting arrangements. A divorce is the literal, legal dissolution of your marriage by way of an order signed by a judge. The divorce is the (somewhat expensive) piece of paper that you get at the end, only once all other issues have been addressed.

Plenty of folks who are not legally married share lives and children. The law often refers to those spouses as *common law*. The definition of *common law* and the length of cohabitation needed for a common-law relationship vary from province to province. But common law or married, the end result if you split up is the same: you will have finances to deal with and parenting arrangements to make. In both cases, we refer to the period between splitting up and, if you were married, obtaining a divorce as a *separation*. If you were common law when you separated, you simply remain separated until your marital status changes (i.e., if you become common law with another person or get married), if at all, in the future. I am careful not to use the words *separation* and *divorce* interchangeably because they mean very different things.

From an equity perspective as well, plenty of (too many) families were, and in many places continue to be, denied the right to formalize their commitment with a legally recognized marriage. This does not make them any less a family, and it does not change the types of issues they face when they separate or make the process any less difficult.

Finding Your Team

Your marriage was likely supported by friends and family, a church affiliation, mentors, a coach, or a therapist. If you were lucky, you had a support system, whatever that looked like.

Your separation or divorce shouldn't be different. And if you had no support during your relationship, it's only fair that at its end you should have all the support in the world.

Navigating these processes is challenging — even for me, and I do it every day.

The best advice from Deborah Graham, a very experienced family law lawyer and pioneer of the collaborative law movement in Toronto, is to tell separating and divorcing parents to choose a team that represents them *as people*; don't seek out the highest priced, prize-fighting lawyer. Find the person who touts solutions-based thinking, negotiated settlements, and respectful dialogue.

In much the same way your wedding photographer wasn't also your hairstylist and cake baker, your separation or divorce may require a multi-disciplinary approach. And that's okay. A divorce that doesn't leave you broke or filled with venom is an investment in your mental health, your future, and the futures of your kids.

What do you want those futures to look like?

GETTING LEGAL ADVICE

While you are allowed to represent yourself in a family law matter (and some people do), I really don't recommend it. At least do yourself the favour of getting legal advice first. You should understand, with clarity, your rights and obligations and which options seem best suited to the specifics of *your family*. You should have all of your questions answered, and you should never rely on Google, your neighbour, or your cousin's sister-in-law for that.

Knowing your rights and obligations is both empowering and integral to setting your expectations. Setting your expectations should be the first step: knowing what is and is not possible is eye-opening and sometimes humbling. Lonny Balbi, QC, a senior family law lawyer in Calgary, Alberta, says that the first meeting with your lawyer will be the most important meeting you have.

Mr. Balbi says that, most often, he recommends mediation to separating partners to address the issues arising from the breakdown of their relationship. He advises this from the perspective of a professional who acts both as a neutral third-party mediator or arbitrator and as a lawyer who represents his own clients in mediation proceedings. He tells his clients that mediation is clearly the best for them. He jokes that a trial is, of course, best for him: he will make more money. But he recommends mediation because it is best for his clients and their families.

When looking for a lawyer to consult with, ask around — you probably have friends or family members who have received family law counsel in the past. Ask them if they loved their lawyers. Did they feel supported and protected? Did their lawyer get things done? Did their lawyer have their best interests at heart?

Try to stay away from online reviews. I can tell you from first-hand experience that many are actually written by the opposing party who feels like they "lost." Online reviews vary so dramatically that it's hard to believe two different reviews could even be about the same person. A reliable resource is the Best Lawyers website, a peer-reviewed guide to lawyers across Canada, in every practice area (see chapter 12). Google lawyers you're contemplating consulting with and see if they have posted any videos they've made or articles they've written, or something else that could offer a glimpse into that lawyer as a person.

Once you've narrowed it down to a few people, have a consultation. Or hey, have a couple. Consultations are generally billed at a lawyer's hourly rate, and some lawyers even charge a flat fee for consultations, usually for about an hour. Information is invaluable and, contrary to popular belief, you can't get all the information online. Family law in each province is highly nuanced, and in some instances it's case-specific. Try not to go down the online rabbit hole — you'll only disappoint yourself.

Just get the information straight from the source and save yourself the headache.

Finding a lawyer you *actually like* is also very important. In my experience, the adage that people hire lawyers who are like them rings true. So find someone who shares your values, feels like they would be a strong advocate should you need one, and seems like a generally kind person who makes you feel calm but reins you in when you need it.

Ask the lawyer what they think about parenting and shared parenting. If their answers sound like what you've been thinking but didn't have words for, they could be a good choice for you.

GETTING THE MOST FROM YOUR CONSULTATION(S)

Come prepared for your consultation.

- Have a decent grip on your income, your spouse's income, and the approximate values of your biggest assets and debts, if you can. Have an idea of what a future schedule for your kids might look like. Bring a list of the questions that have been keeping you up at night.
- Bring someone you trust to your consults. Most lawyers are totally fine with this. I tell everyone that this is a kind of meeting you've likely never had in your life, on a subject you know very little about, so a second pair of ears is really helpful. And having them to talk to afterward is also useful. Decompressing and evaluating options is better with two heads.
- Take notes during your consultation. You are not going to remember everything. In fact, these meetings have a tendency to be emotionally charged and confusing, especially if it is very early post-separation. Write down things that are important to you and things that you were surprised to learn.
- If finances are an issue, as they are for so many people, see chapter 12 for places to get free or cheap(er) legal advice, access to court-run mediation programs, and many other forms of support.
- Ask those questions on your list, and then ask follow-up questions if you don't understand or the answers bring up

more questions. This is normal. You're not supposed to know everything.

- Don't leave out any details of your story that you feel are embarrassing or paint you in a negative light. Your lawyer has, quite literally, seen it all. It's important for them to know the story so that they are prepared for whatever may come up down the road.

- Remember that it is your lawyer's job to encourage all approaches to out-of-court settlement. Lawyers are also required to encourage, or at least flesh out the possibility of, reconciliation. That's why they will bring it up often, to the point that you might find it annoying. Remember that an out-of-court settlement is usually — probably 99 percent of the time — what is best for your family.

- Keep in mind that it is also your lawyer's job to prepare for the worst-case scenario (that is, going to court, or going to trial, which is the ultimate in court appearances). That doesn't mean you'll ever come close to finding yourself there, but it does mean that if you do, you'll be ready for it. For example, when dealing with financial issues like child or spousal support or property division, your lawyer will insist on a complete and detailed financial disclosure from each of you. You may wonder why all the invasive, personal questions. Well, again, if you end up in court in the future, your lawyer wants to be armed with *all* the information they need. And if you're negotiating a settlement, the standard for disclosure is the same: a lawyer will not be able to advise you on proposed settlement terms without being able to discuss with you, in a high-level way, precisely what you are giving up or walking away from.

FINDING A MEDIATOR, PARENTING MEDIATOR, OR OTHER PROFESSIONAL

The lawyer you consult with, and the lawyer you might hire, will readily recommend a parenting mediator, parenting coordinator, parenting coach, family therapist, or other professional who, if required, will play a large role in your case, also called a *file*. In all likelihood, the lawyer will recommend someone with whom they have a previous working relationship, professional rapport, and trust.

The lawyer will take that a step further. For example, if it's a mediator you need, the lawyer will recommend one, or a few, based on the facts of your specific case. If the issues are largely about parenting, a person experienced in that area will be recommended. If the issues are predominantly about numbers, a person who is talented and creative with numbers will be called on. My advice is to take the lawyer's recommendations. They will be honest with you.

FINDING A MENTAL HEALTH ADVOCATE

Find a mental health practitioner if you don't already have one involved in your care. I say this many times (so many that it will get annoying), and I say it because it is so important. Picture me screaming it from a rooftop, through a tinny megaphone. Mental health *is* health. Having strategies to cope with times of high tension (which are often part of the process) and implementing those strategies in real-life settings will make a world of difference for you.

While there are many, many ways to access mental health support, the path can be hard to navigate. It's really easy for me to say, "Find a great therapist!" but there are lots of working parts in the process. The value of mental health support cannot be quantified, yet many people experience lack of accessibility. People of colour, and specifically those identifying as women and mothers, often encounter discrimination in accessing mental health services. Their concerns may be disregarded or downplayed, and when they can access services, their generational trauma is often not acknowledged. Similarly, members of the LGBTQ2S+ community experience barriers to accessing support, as do those with low incomes. In other words, the therapy that works for an upper- or middle-class, cisgender, straight white person doesn't work for most others. This is not intended to slight the work of therapists but rather to acknowledge that therapy is complex and that cultural awareness and understanding — a personal understanding of the barriers faced by clients — makes a difference in what those clients gain from the therapy services.

In 2020, Black Mental Health Matters, the first-ever organization of its kind in the Toronto area, was born. As stated on its website, the organization "caters to clients who typically can't afford mental health services, and provides low cost treatment options, when needed, with a therapist who is culturally understanding." Services like these are severely lacking but absolutely necessary, serving a tremendous purpose now and into the future. More information is found in chapter 12.

Therapy comes in many formats and is delivered many ways. For psychotherapy, the kind of talk therapy you often see on television shows and the most common form of therapy, you do not need a referral from your doctor. You are free to find your own therapist, and you should use similar criteria as in your lawyer search: Do they come recommended? Did previous clients feel supported and protected or did they feel censored? Did the client emerge with tools to apply to day-to-day life? Did they feel that the therapist understood their cultural- or religious-specific circumstances and traumas? Did they feel they could relate to the therapist? In chapter 12, you will find many resources for therapy services, including cultural-specific ones.

Psychotherapy is not inexpensive: the going rate is typically from $100 to $150 per one-hour session and is sometimes much more. While some extended health-care benefits packages, if you are fortunate enough to have one, may cover some or all of these types of expenses, some don't. But if you can support the expense, psychotherapy can be a sound investment. Indeed, it has helped me to navigate all sorts of tricky circumstances in my life.

Psychotherapists, therapists, and counsellors come from different walks of life. Most are registered social workers who possess a master's degree or doctorate in social work. They are trained to identify and assess mental health problems and to provide strategies for coping with those problems and for improving them, over time. They cannot prescribe medication and their services are often paid for out-of-pocket.

In contrast, services provided by a psychologist may be covered by provincial or territorial health plans, extended health-care benefits, or insurance, and they may require a referral from your family medical care provider. Often, that's the best place to start: talking to your doctor. They can make the referrals required, but if they know you are struggling with your mental health, they will also keep tabs on you and will be there if you require support or information.

Psychologists are not medical doctors. Their expertise includes psychological testing and assessment of emotional and cognitive functions, the diagnosis of emotional and cognitive disorders, and the use of evidence-based psychological treatments and psychotherapies. Most people who work with a psychologist do so for a short time, rather than long-term for their ongoing mental health support.

Psychiatrists, on the other hand, are medical doctors with a specialty in the diagnosis and treatment of mental illnesses. You will need a referral from your family doctor to see a psychiatrist. The biggest difference between a psychiatrist and other therapy providers (therapist, counsellor, social worker, or psychologist) and is that a psychiatrist *can* prescribe medications such as antidepressants and anti-anxiety mediations to support your recovery, and they will monitor you along the way.

FINDING A SUPPORT GROUP

The gaps between therapy sessions can be long, as therapists often have long client lists and wait times between sessions. Another excellent tool is a support group. There are support groups for everything. Some are formal groups led by a mental health professional, while others are more casual groups of peers. There are resources online and on social media sites that you can tap into. You can find support groups through members of your support team or through community health organizations. And, like all good things, you can ask around your network. Chances are, someone has attended, or is attending, a support group for issues similar to yours. The Canadian Mental Health Association also has lots of excellent resources (see chapter 12).

Plenty of similarly aged, like-minded folks are going through exactly what you're going through, and having people to commiserate with is so important. Look for a group that works well for you; don't just go with the first one you come across. Find a place that feels safe and supportive — you'll know quickly whether it's a good fit or not.

FINDING A DIVORCE FINANCIAL PROFESSIONAL

If household finances, budgeting, and retirement planning are not your thing, or if you are about to find yourself responsible for managing them for the first time, find a *certified divorce financial analyst* (also called a *certified divorce financial planner*). You might want to work with them now, to compile your financial disclosure, or in the future, for budgeting, retirement planning, tax planning, and other financial advice. It's important to remember that from a financial perspective, as much as you want the process to be over, even to the point of being willing to make a deal for less than you may be entitled to, you have many, many years ahead of you and you need to plan for those, too. And those years should be happy ones.

FINDING A DIVORCE COACH

If you need more day-to-day support than your lawyer can reasonably provide, you can look for a divorce coach, divorce doula, or divorce consultant. Despite the titles, they are not restricted to working with people who hold a marriage certificate; they can work with unmarried spouses, too. They offer services such as pre-divorce planning (when you are contemplating a separation or divorce but have not yet taken steps toward one), separation coaching, hostile dynamics management coaching (providing skills to cope with emotional abuse), preparing terms for a parenting plan or separation agreement, and assisting with understanding personal and family finances, including budget planning, future expenses, and retirement. They also provide guidance in preparing for court appearances or meetings with lawyers; lawyers are much more expensive than divorce coaches, and the more prepared you are and the more wisely you use your lawyer's time, the more economical it will be.

And they don't just deal with the business aspects of divorce and separation. Divorce coaches can also help you in blending families in the future, in coping with your new spouse's hostile ex-partner, in step-parenting, and so on.

■

I know this feels like a lot, and I've probably brought up issues you didn't even have on your radar. But once you've done the hard work of putting your team together, you'll receive the valuable support you need. Set yourself up for success. In a separation or divorce, the goal isn't just to come out of it in one piece. It's to emerge with confidence and support, ready for the next steps.

The First Legal Step

Often, when (if) you formally retain a lawyer to act on your behalf, the logical first step is for them to write a letter to your former spouse, or to their lawyer if they have one. I've written countless such letters. The letter will let the other person or their lawyer know that you have retained a lawyer of your own (or that you'll be acting on your own behalf, if you choose to). It will let them know, usually, that you wish to settle the issues as amicably and cost-effectively as possible. In other words, this is how to inform your former spouse or their lawyer that you want to negotiate an out-of-court settlement.

Of course, it doesn't always *end up* that way, but most files start off on this foot.

You may wish to deal with your file in pieces, first addressing child-related issues, which are often the most pressing. If so, you or your lawyer will let your former spouse or their lawyer know that you want to negotiate a parenting plan first and focus on the financial issues later. As long as you have sorted out your living arrangements (even if they are temporary until, for example, your family home has been sold or transferred to one of you), you can negotiate a parenting plan and a residential schedule that best suits the kids' needs.

More and more families are choosing to address their family law matters in this way: focusing on the issues in order of importance to them. In my experience, because parenting issues are often the most sensitive ones for newly separated parents, resolving them first can pave the way for successful, and relatively short, negotiations on all the other issues. When the most important issues are no longer on the table, the intensity of emotions people experience seem to be reduced, and other issues just don't seem to matter as much when things are calmer.

There are exceptions to every rule, and certainly what I've outlined above is not always the case, but with willing participants, it often can be.

Stephanie is a divorced parent of one kid, now eight years old.

When she and her ex split, she admits, she went in with guns blazing. She was angry at him. Life with him had been a string of disappointments until she'd finally had the courage to end the relationship, on her terms. But as she chose her own happiness, more stability, more financial predictability, and less strife, he fought back at every turn.

Stephanie wanted the best for their daughter, but she conflated what was best for their daughter with what was best for herself.

Instead of moving on and enjoying her life more, she spent the first long while fighting over nothing, and she spent tens of thousands of dollars doing so.

Looking back, she says she would have done everything differently. "If you're going to spend any money on your divorce," she says, "hire the best mediator you can and stay away from court. God, what a waste of money that was."

3

Working Toward a Resolution: Picking Your Settlement Process(es)

CHOOSING A PROCESS IS THE NEXT MOST IMPORTANT STEP. MOST people are not aware of all the options available to them and may find the details confusing, rightfully so. There can be a great deal of overlap, but the objectives of the processes are all pretty much the same: resolution.

Here are my notes on the various avenues for dispute resolution, in order from my most favourite to my least:

Negotiation

Negotiation is exactly what it sounds like: working out a solution to the issues between you and your former spouse. This can be done directly between the two of you, but I highly recommend negotiating through your respective lawyers.

Here, you and your ex retain power over your own lives — and I like that, because I'm a Libra. Co-operation is key. And a strong understanding that you will never "win," that you'll never, ever get everything you want, exactly the way you want it, goes a long way toward finding a resolution.

In order to successfully negotiate, you need to enter the process armed with all the information you need, whether from your consultations with lawyers or from a lawyer retained to act on your behalf. You also need a wish list of the things you'd really like to have, including those priorities that are not tangible, like peace and calm.

Every single issue arising from the breakdown of your relationship can have a negotiated resolution: parenting, child support, spousal support, property — all of it. With willing participants who have received good advice and have good support in place, anything is possible in negotiations.

I am a huge proponent of learning the rules before you break them. Family law, thankfully, is rather formulaic when it comes to money issues — that is, spousal support (often referred to as alimony on American TV shows), child support, and the division of property — for both married and unmarried spouses. Depending on the province or territory you reside in, relatively simple mathematical formulas and federally legislated guidelines dictate what the outcomes of these issues are likely to look like. Knowing your rights and entitlements is of the utmost importance, and knowing points of leverage can come in handy when negotiations get tough. Going into the process of negotiation with a clear picture of what your best-day and worst-day scenarios look like is invaluable. Guidance from your team will help you obtain this clear picture.

A cost-benefit analysis is important, too. By now, you know that if you go to court about a certain issue; and you have a compelling backstory, solid legal arguments, and a sympathetic, energetic judge; and it's a sunny and unusually quiet day in the courthouse and the wind is blowing in a certain direction (you see where I'm going here?), you could "win" on the issue. But what astronomical sum of money did it cost you to get there? And how will you pay for it? Most of the lawyers I interviewed for this book, all senior family law practitioners across Canada, suggested that the average cost of bringing a motion before a judge — *one* singular court appearance in which you are allowed to make legal arguments and the judge decides what the outcome should be — is about $15,000. Plus tax. Imagine the far more enjoyable things you could do with $15,000.

The vast majority of families I work with end up with a negotiated settlement. That's not to say they don't have to threaten court — or sometimes even start a court action — to get there, but most of them decide to take control of their own outcomes, and they work together toward the objective of a comprehensive plain-language agreement that governs how the issues between them will be addressed. Much of the time, where children are involved, a substantial portion of the separation agreement deals with a significant number of child-related issues. The goal is to leave the process with a document that will carry the family through the next several years without the need to continually revisit the terms or argue about them. The agreement is meant to pave the way for easier communication and more routine, consistency, and predictability because, simply, everyone thrives on that.

It's vital to know this: when it comes to a negotiated settlement, *you are in charge.* Between the two of you, you can decide what each should pay, who should live where, and where and when the children should live with each of you. The settlement does not have to perfectly abide by the law to be put in place. It's your family, and these are your choices. Please don't ever lose sight of that, even if you lose your footing somewhere along the line.

If your former spouse is willing to engage in respectful dialogue and has the same objectives as you, more or less, you are absolutely allowed to hammer out an agreement without lawyers representing you. But before you make it final, bring it to a lawyer. As Adam Black, a lawyer in Toronto, puts it, "It's not simply a matter of rubber-stamping it. There are plenty of scenarios you probably haven't thought of." And by that he means do you have provisions in your agreement for where the kids spend Christmas morning? What about their birthdays? What about your birthdays? What expenses are too expensive when it comes to the kids? What if one person wants to move fifty kilometres away but still share equal time with the kids? We often forget to look forward when we're desperately trying to address the things happening before our eyes. These agreements are meant to last for the foreseeable future. Not forever, but for some time.

It's important to take your agreement to someone who is experienced with these types of settlements, someone who reads them every day and helps folks negotiate and navigate their terms. That person will be invaluable to you and will offer insight that comes with experience. Chances are this is your first divorce, but it's probably their four thousandth.

You won't spend $15,000 doing this, but every dollar you allocate will be a sage investment in your future and that of your kids. Protecting your interests and maintaining the peace and calm that comes with an executed separation agreement is worth the time and effort — and is something worth celebrating. An achievement, if you will.

Another reason you need to take your agreement to a lawyer is that, if you have represented yourself (that is, worked without a lawyer formally retained on your behalf), you are required to have independent legal advice before you sign it. If the lawyer thinks you're making a bad deal, they'll tell you. If they think the terms are prejudicial or unfair, they'll tell you that, too. Ultimately, their job is to protect you, but they also have an obligation to protect themselves. Occasionally, clients who just want the ordeal to be over will sign any document to end the process and obtain what they feel, in that moment, is closure. But a few years later, they come back upset about one term or another that has to be contended with. Good lawyers are skilled at identifying folks who may be signing an agreement under duress, or who may be otherwise compromised. They will ask you questions about your agreement, how you arrived at the terms, and why you agreed to certain things. If they are satisfied that you absolutely, unequivocally understand the impact of what you are signing, they will provide independent legal advice and sign off on the agreement, usually as your witness as well. But they have to be sure first. So make sure you have an agreement you can live with for a long time, not just to the end of the week.

Mediation

More and more lawyers are recommending mediation and offering it as a service themselves. Mediation is a tool used with great success in family law matters. Mediators can address financial, parenting, and property issues. They can address all the issues or only specific ones as dictated by you. It may be that you've been able to achieve a negotiated settlement on some issues but find yourselves at a stalemate on others (that's normal, I promise!). Mediation is excellent at smashing through those barriers; I've seen it work beautifully time and again and only rarely fail, even in situations of high conflict. Even for couples who were, in the beginning, hell-bent on going to court.

Mediation is a *voluntary* process. No one is obliged to participate, and anyone can leave if they feel that the process isn't working.

As with negotiated settlements, in mediation you've got creative licence. You and your former spouse can literally storyboard the next several years of your lives if you want to. Frame by frame, you can creatively resolve things without having to adhere to the law at every turn, as long as you understand the law and what it *would* likely provide for you if you went to court (again, we use this metric to plan for worst-case scenarios). A good, responsible family law lawyer will typically tell you what the law would give you, so that if you settle on "less" than that, you know what you're potentially giving up. A good, responsible family mediator will ensure that everyone understands everything.

MEDIATING THE PARENTING ISSUES

A *parenting mediator* assists the parents on a limited basis to resolve all parenting issues. A *parenting coordinator* is engaged by the parents on a longer-term basis to help enforce the terms of the parenting agreement or separation agreement. A parenting mediator is often a lawyer but sometimes is not and may also be a mental health professional. They have a wealth of knowledge about parenting and children's best interests. Parents know their children best, and the professional working as a parenting mediator or parenting coordinator knows how to get co-parents where they need to go. A parenting coordinator can come from a mix of professional backgrounds.

Most of the family law lawyers I interviewed expressed the same sentiment: when you have kids, your money is best spent on a parenting mediator. Once those most sensitive, triggering issues of where and how the children will live are addressed, the other issues become much easier, for the most part.

These professionals work with prospective co-parents to achieve a stand-alone document called a *parenting plan*. They usually don't touch financial issues or examine bank accounts. Parties often work directly with this person, with their lawyers quietly waiting in the background for updates and answering questions that relate to their individual client's rights and obligations.

Domestic Violence, Intimate Partner Violence, and Power Imbalance Screening

Parties to a potential mediation are always screened for domestic violence, abuse, and power imbalances, and mediators are trained to seek out signs of these problems. Most often, a power imbalance is created when there is domestic violence or intimate partner violence in the relationship, whether past or present.

This sometimes means, unfortunately, that two people who are otherwise willing may not be deemed candidates for mediation because the mediator has genuine concerns that one party can be coerced into a settlement they don't really want. However, and this point is important, with the right lawyers involved, mediation can still be possible when domestic violence or intimate partner violence is deemed to be present. In these circumstances, it's about ascertaining whether the person who has suffered abuse (and, sometimes, that is both people) can feel safe in the environment created by the mediator and the lawyers. If the parties feel safe and supported, they can still consent to a mediated process if that is what they want, and a mediated resolution is still possible.

Thankfully — because mediation is an excellent alternative to other available options — most parties are candidates for mediation.

Statistics Canada found in 2018 that more than four in every ten persons identifying as women have been victims of intimate partner violence in their lifetimes, and one-third of persons identifying as men have experienced intimate partner violence in their lifetimes. There are three main categories of domestic and intimate partner violence: psychological, physical, and sexual.

Psychological violence is difficult to detect because it has few, if any, outward signs that an untrained eye could identify. One form is financial abuse and control, such as not allowing the other person to have their own bank account, credit card, or bank debit card. Examples of other forms of psychological violence include put-downs, name-calling, stalking, harassing, following, jealousy, manipulation, confinement, and property damage. During screening, it is important to be open and honest with the mediator. It is for your own safety; being victimized is nothing to be ashamed of.

Physical domestic violence often goes unreported to authorities, for a variety of infuriating reasons related to broken systems that fail victims at every turn. But unreported does not equal unimportant. Hitting, kicking, biting, assaulting with a weapon, threatening with violence or a weapon, and death threats are all types of physical violence.

If, during the screening process, you report any type of violence toward your children, it will be reported to the appropriate people or agencies. Your lawyer, therapist, and other members of your team are usually professionally obligated to their governing bodies to report any violence against children that is reported to them in order to ensure the children's safety.

Parenting plans are true works of art dedicated to setting the framework for seamless, predictable co-parenting. They examine all possible scenarios and address them accordingly. Often, the parenting plan will later be appended to the separation agreement, which addresses the other issues arising from the breakdown of your relationship, to demonstrate how parenting is to be handled.

While parenting mediation is an incredibly useful tool, it is relatively new. When I began my career, it was rare to see parties attend mediation strictly to address parenting. Back then, all the issues were viewed as a package deal. Your lawyer is undoubtedly intelligent and insightful and may even be a parent themselves. But they're not child development experts and sometimes they are not mediators. More often than not, crafting parenting plans between lawyers can get very expensive, very quickly.

A good parenting mediator is an excellent use of your resources. They can often check every box on both parents' to-do lists in just one or two sessions and then provide you with a draft parenting plan for your review. In some cases, you may even leave a parenting mediation session with a signed agreement in hand.

Mediation, whether to address parenting or other family law issues, is voluntary. This means that both parties have to be ready and willing to come to the table, to listen, and to be flexible. They have to know what their best- and worst-day scenarios are, and they need to recognize that no one emerges victorious; there will be things they give and things they get.

OPEN VERSUS CLOSED MEDIATION

Mediation can be open, or it can be closed. In open mediation, if everything falls apart and the mediation is unsuccessful, the parties can share details about the mediation in future settings or with a judge in court. This includes details of settlement discussions, the parties' positions in mediation, and their respective behaviours throughout. In closed mediation, neither party can discuss or share any information resulting from mediation. Depending on the facts of the case, it may be detrimental if the mediation is open, or if it is closed. The parties' lawyers will often recommend one over the other for a particular case, but ultimately the clients decide what's best.

If it's successful, mediation will conclude in much the same way a negotiation does, with a detailed *memorandum of understanding* (or minutes of settlement, or separation agreement, or parenting plan). This will often provide the framework for drafting a comprehensive separation agreement.

Mediation-Arbitration

In certain cases, parties will add a layer to their mediation process by agreeing that it will be a mediation-arbitration process (or "medi-arb"). The addition of arbitration is like a second line of defence. In medi-arb, the parties agree in advance that if they are unable to reach a deal with their mediator within a set number of sessions or hours, and if they find themselves at an impasse that cannot be conquered, the mediator they mutually chose then has arbitral powers. This means the mediator has the ability to make a binding decision, referred to as an *award*, much like a judge making a court order. They will arbitrate (that is, decide) the issues for the parties that they have been unable to decide on their own.

I like mediation-arbitration and the finality it implies. I like that the looming threat of arbitration — of having your liberties effectively clawed back just long enough for the mediator-arbitrator to decide on your behalf — keeps parties in check, for the most part. I like that the mediator-arbitrator is agreed upon in advance and that they already have insight into the family dynamic, because you have worked with them, likely extensively, to that point. You do not need to start fresh in a new venue, and now a decision will be made for you.

Sitting in on many mediation sessions, I have learned a great deal. One of the best mediators I know preferred to start his sessions in the loveliest and most unexpected way. At the beginning of the first session with new clients, he would ask the two parties to come together in one room so he could introduce himself. Having read their materials and gained an understanding of what he was getting into, he would start with something personal: "Look at how successful your kids are," or "Tell me about your kids." He would do this even when the issues before him were not, on the face of them, child-related. A lot of folks would be taken aback. His intent was to humanize the process; to remind nervous, anxious, or angry participants about what mattered most; and to gently affirm that despite this being such a significant time in the clients' lives, it was also nothing special. He'd seen it before, and he'd see it again.

He would always start on a positive note and hope to keep it that way. There was a reason he was so wildly successful, and this approach, I am sure, was a tremendous part of that.

Collaborative Family Law

The *collaborative family law practice model* is an interesting one. I learned about it in Toronto, around 2006 or so. It popped up in a few Hollywood movies, like *The Kids Are All Right*, and from there people ran with the idea.

I can understand why. The cornerstones of collaborative practice or collaborative divorce are mutual respect and co-operation. Parties agree, in advance, to enter a negotiated process in which they will not slander each other; will not yell, scream, or belittle each other; and will act calmly and respectfully toward one another. Usually, although not always, they are each accompanied by their own legal representatives who have undertaken extensive collaborative law training and subscribe to the principles of *collaborative family law*. If there is significant conflict or complicated financial issues, collaborative practice promotes a multidisciplinary approach, and a financial professional or mental health professional (or both) trained in collaborative family practice may also be engaged. Collaborative family law practitioners tend to be passionate about their approach, and they are usually very child-focused as well.

Before the parties and their lawyers dive in, they will sign a collaborative law *participation agreement* that affirms the three principles on which collaborative family law is based:

1. The parties agree in advance to voluntarily exchange complete financial information, meaning nothing is missing, intentionally omitted, or understated.

2. The parties make a pledge to stay in this process and to avoid court.

3. The parties agree to conduct themselves respectfully and to achieve a resolution by way of a separation agreement or some other form of domestic contract.

Here is where collaborative law differs dramatically from other forms of dispute resolution: in every other voluntary process, there is that ominous elephant in the room tapping you on the shoulder and reminding you it's there: *court*. You can go to court at any time if things fall apart. You can go at one person's whim; even if the other person doesn't want to, they are obliged to respond.

In collaborative practice, you are signing up for something very different. If the process fails (which it sometimes does, for various reasons — nothing is perfect), you have to give up your lawyers, who are already quite invested timewise and financially in your file. They know the details of your lives and are acquainted with the two of you as people. If you opt for litigation, your lawyers are done. It's like another breakup. You will now need to hire a family law lawyer who does litigation and effectively start again from the bottom — which includes the significant cost of bringing someone new up to speed. A helpful collaborative lawyer will do everything they can to ease the transition, but your new lawyer will need to take the time to review your file to this point and determine what has and has not been accomplished.

This is a potential downside to collaborative practice that you need to be aware of, but it's meant as a deterrent. No one wants to spend money on a process only to have to start all over again, but some parties end up there anyway.

The other major difference from other forms of voluntary dispute resolution is the food. Yes! You read that right. Collaborative family law meetings have snacks. Way more food than four adults who either have already eaten or can't because their stomach is in knots will ever need. Cookies, croissants, sandwiches, crudités and dip! Snacks abound. The idea is that people will put in the work if they're not starving and their blood sugar is stable. If everyone is working diligently and snacks are available, you can keep going without breaks. Some lawyers do this really fancy-like, and some put out a tin of Royal Dansk cookies. I'm not discerning. I love snacks.

> When my boss asked a client what was the worst thing their ex would say about them, the client answered that they had secretly spent half a million dollars.
>
> On an escort.
>
> Seeing us raise our eyebrows in shock, the client said, "But you don't get it — she was hot!"
>
> All this is to say that we've heard it all, and even the messiest, most complicated matters can be settled out of court. Negotiating a settlement — actually playing a starring role in deciding some of the biggest changes that will take place in your life — is by far preferable to having a stranger who doesn't know you, or your kids, make that decision for you.
>
> When you're reading the next chapter, I want you to keep that in mind. Nothing is impossible, and you don't have to go down the road to court if you can avoid it.

4

So You Want to Go to Court, Huh?: Litigation as a Last Resort

SO, IF YOU'VE READ THIS FAR, I NEED YOU TO STOP BEFORE GOING any further and ask yourself why the hell you would want to go to court. Consider these questions:

1. Is it your only option?
2. Is your trusted adviser recommending this as the best course of action based on the variables of your unique family law matter?
3. Are you doing it for the right reasons? Yes, this is a loaded question. If you just want to stick it to someone, you will absolutely achieve that through a court experience. However, *you* will suffer, too. And your kids will remember it.
4. Do you know everything there is to know about the court process and the potential costs (which can never be fully appreciated until you've paid your last bill)?
5. Do you know how long it can take?
6. Are you prepared to have a complete stranger make decisions for you and your family?
7. Is there currently a declared pandemic? (Ha, ha.)

If you answered yes to any of these questions and there are young children involved, try to find a better way. If you said yes to more than one question, I want you to go through the list again and really think. How much of your answer is rooted in anger or sadness or frustration? Is this something you will regret in the future, when you will inevitably feel much differently than you do now?

This is the stuff that people think about when they think about family law — *Marriage Story* for my generation, *The War of the Roses* for my mom's. It's the stuff that keeps people up at night when they're contemplating a separation or a divorce, or when one is dropped into their laps unexpectedly. From the excessive delays to the tremendous cost, court is not for the faint of heart. That's not to say that it doesn't have its place; it is an integral part of the family law sphere and another tool in the family law tool box. But it sucks.

Court

It's some scary shit. I've been there, in support of other people and as a witness for a friend in a family law case. I've taken notes and carried file boxes and organized exhibits to be entered into evidence. Court is intimidating, from the oversized placard hanging above the bench of the cartoon lion and unicorn cradling a coat of arms that actually reads *Evil to him who thinks evil*, to the 1980s' microphones, the muted tones of the beige walls, the cracking paint, and the dirty carpet and brown furniture. None of it is conducive to making a person feel comfortable, which is precisely the point. We're not supposed to feel at home there.

I hate it. All of it.

But don't worry, the court doesn't like you, either.

There are intentionally built-in delays from the time you file an application — the document that incites an action and the thing people often mean when they talk about "divorce papers." It could be six weeks or more before you set foot in a courtroom, and sometimes even longer.

One of the major things that sets court apart from all other forms of dispute resolution is that court is involuntary. Once an action is started, you do not have the luxury of ignoring it.

So why do we end up there if we hate it so much? Good question.

You see, sometimes when two people really love each other and that goes south and they split up, they will start out on the right foot. They'll exchange financial disclosure and proposals about how to share the kids' time between their homes. And then? Nothing. Radio silence. Despite many follow-ups and promises to send a disclosure along or to respond to proposals or whatever is needed, nothing happens. But each time a follow-up letter or email goes from one lawyer to the other, the lawyers are getting paid. You can see how quickly that adds up when lawyers' rates are several hundred dollars per hour.

Starting a court action is often viewed as a last resort. It may be pursued when a person just cannot elicit a timely response from the other, whether through their lawyer or not; in rare cases when a legal action has to be started on an emergency basis; or when a party pretends to want to negotiate but only on their terms (meaning, of course, that no negotiating is happening).

When you start a court action, the other person (who becomes the "other party" once litigation has begun) is given a narrow window of time to respond to your claims. In Ontario, it's just thirty days. If the other party doesn't meet the deadline, you can take all kinds of steps, if you want to spend the money to do so. Most people respond within the prescribed window when they realize they're not in charge anymore, or they retain a lawyer, who contacts the lawyer on the other side to set a new timetable on consent. Being served with court documents is a rude awakening and usually lights the fire needed to get things going. Sometimes, it is what it takes for the other person to understand how serious their spouse is about moving forward.

Litigation lasts months and months, or sometimes years. I once worked on a file that was in and out of court for nine years. Nine. It only ended because our client died. Literally. And then their former spouse went on to sue the client's estate.

Nothing is quick or simple. There is a prescribed sequence of court appearances (discussed below), each focused on turning you away. A judge will offer their best advice on how to settle the issues between the two of you. If you come back a few months later having apparently not listened to that advice, you'll have some explaining to do.

In my experience, most people who start a court action end up settling outside of court anyway. Usually, the experience of preparing a claim and then preparing for the first appearance before a judge, as well as the associated costs, take the wind out of a litigant's sails. I like it when this happens, because I feel relieved for the two people who were about to borrow against their futures to fund further court appearances.

Reality Check

One of the most difficult parts of this work is managing peoples' expectations about what can and cannot and will and will not be accomplished in court. One of the hardest truths for clients is that our laws and courtrooms don't tend to care about the details: how much one parent worked versus how much the other parented, or didn't, during the marriage or relationship doesn't matter. The things we are so sure will give us a "win" actually don't make the other person a worse parent. And when it comes to parenting specifically, it doesn't matter who had the spending problem or the weird relationship with their mother. If none of those "faults" inhibits a person's ability to parent, that person should continue to spend time with their children, as often as possible and definitely as much as the other parent.

Divorce in Canada is "no fault," like car insurance. No amount of cheating or lying or overspending will get you more or less of what you believe you're entitled to. The court wants facts, not anecdotal evidence. And it'll usually be very quick — almost curt — to tell you that.

Clients find this jarring, the abruptness with which some judges will announce that something doesn't matter or isn't germane to the issues. It, rightfully, scares clients away and oftentimes guides them to another path when they realize court is not how it's portrayed on TV.

For the approximately 1 percent (really, it's that low!) of people who end up in court for the long haul, or to the point of concluding a family law trial, it is exhausting in every possible way, and expensive. You may not receive a decision from the judge's chambers until months and months, or sometimes years, after a trial has concluded — leaving you hanging in the meantime. And much like with the other methods of resolution, no one really ever wins. When you finally do get that decision, it may not even be the decision you wanted.

And the notion of simply appealing a decision because you don't like it or you think the judge made an error? Yeah, sure, it's possible. But in the time it'll take, your kids will become adults and the decision won't matter anymore. Time is truly precious and the Venn diagram of family law litigation and the timespan of childhood only overlaps at loss. Lost time. Lost childhoods. Lost money. Lost opportunities to cultivate good, strong parenting relationships that will see your children through all kinds of situations life will throw at them.

No one was ever going to win in court.

Federal Legislation and Divorce

The *Divorce Act* is a piece of federal legislation that applies to legally *married* spouses only. For those couples, the act addresses parenting time and decision-making responsibility, the division of property, child support, spousal support, and divorce. Additionally, each province and territory has its own provincial legislation relating to family law and children. Ontario, for example, has the *Family Law Act* and the *Children's Law Reform Act*.

In 2021 the federal *Divorce Act* underwent significant changes to its language related to parenting, removing words like *custody* and *access* from the family law vernacular, and provided a much clearer definition of intimate partner violence and domestic violence. The changes also introduced guidelines on what *the best interests of the child* means. Determining what is in a child's best interests now includes

- the nature of the child's relationships with each spouse, their siblings, and other important people in their life;
- each spouse's willingness to encourage the child's relationship with the other spouse;
- the child's views and preferences;
- the child's cultural and linguistic upbringing, including the child's Indigenous heritage;
- the ability of each spouse to care for the child;
- the presence of any civil or criminal court actions and orders that are relevant to the well-being of the child; and
- the presence of family violence.

The payment of child support is governed by federal law. The Federal Child Support Guidelines provide not only the framework for determining who owes what for the support of the children and to whom (presented in very easy-to-use tables), but also sets out the degree of financial disclosure that parties are obliged to exchange in order to review child support, which is typically done annually. The guidelines further provide a mathematical formula for determining the percentage to be paid by each parent (referred to as *apportioning*) of the children's extraordinary expenses, such as child care, summer camp, extracurricular activities, and medical and dental expenses not covered by extended health-care benefits.

Spousal support, referred to on American television as *alimony,* is governed by the federal Spousal Support Advisory Guidelines (SSAG), which were drafted by two family law professors with the original intent of being incorporated into the federal *Divorce Act.* The SSAG suggest appropriate ranges of support in a variety of situations for spouses who are entitled to support. The guidelines *do not* provide advice on whether a spouse is entitled to support — you have to get that information from legal counsel, in the form of a consultation or otherwise. A person's right (*entitlement*) to support depends on how the law applies to their specific situation, which is different from your situation, and from your friends' situations; hence the emphasis on getting advice tailored to your own matter.

The SSAG are — surprising to some — not law. However, judges most often base their decisions about spousal support on these guidelines. Many family lawyers also use them when helping clients make decisions and when constructing spousal support agreements in negotiations.

The SSAG provide a range for the monthly payments that one spouse owes the other, from the "low end" to the midpoint to the "high end." A number of factors impact the *quantum* (monthly amount of support payable) and the *duration* (length of time over which the support is payable) of spousal support in Canada. Among those are the recipient's age at the time the parties separated; the length of the relationship (including, in the case of married people, the period of time during which they cohabited before they were married); the age of the youngest child of the relationship and the number of years left before they graduate from high school; and the parties' respective incomes and their abilities to earn income and be self-sufficient.

Overview of Court Process (in Ontario)

The laws governing certain aspects of a family law file vary from province to province to territory in Canada. My experience rests in Ontario. So here I will outline the process we use in Ontario for family law matters. Ontario has the highest-volume family courts, and as I learned in my research, many courts across the country have similar, but different, processes in place.

APPLICATION

If you decide that court is your only option, your first step (other than in limited circumstances) is to *commence an application*, a document applying to the court for various *relief* (court orders) for things you want, like a certain sum of money each month or a specific residential schedule for your kids. Once the application is served on the other party (the *respondent*), they have thirty days to respond with a document called an *answer*. That document serves a few purposes: in it, they respond to your claims (explaining why you're right or wrong), make their own claims, and tell their side of the story.

Once you are served with their answer, you, as the *applicant*, will have a further ten days to respond with a document called a *reply*. This is only necessary if the respondent raises new issues that warrant your response, or if you need to respond to their claims.

CASE CONFERENCE

It usually takes about six weeks (sometimes longer) to go from serving your application to walking into a courtroom for the first in a series of prescribed court appearances. In most courts, we start with a *case conference*. In certain courts, we are required to start with a *first appearance*. A first appearance is a fairly underwhelming appearance in court where the parties identify themselves, confirm that they understand the process and the claims each are making, and introduce their counsel if they have retained someone.

Case conferences are particularly interesting and, indeed, many cases find their way to some kind of resolution following a case conference. Before the case conference, a judge (in many courts in Ontario, a former family law lawyer) will review each party's materials — basically a summary that explains what they want, how things are, how things used to be, how they want things to be, and how they propose to get there. At the case conference, the judge will give you their best advice, based on their experience and the available case law, as to how to settle the issues. But that's all they can do.

At the case conference, the judge is not permitted to make a *substantive order*. This means there's no dramatic tapping of the gavel on the bench and no declaration of what someone is going to do. In fact, most of the time this will never happen, and you also usually don't get a decision from a judge at the end of a court appearance; you usually have to wait for that, too. If there are procedural issues, like the disclosure of documents or completion of expert's reports, preventing the matter from moving forward, the judge is permitted to make a *procedural order* in an attempt to mitigate future delays. A case conference is never what a client expects, no matter how well we explain it to them. Case conferences are often frustrating, sometimes feel unnecessary, and still cost a lot at the end of the day.

Once a case conference has been held, it is said that the issues have now been *canvassed*, meaning the parties are aware of what each wants and where the discrepancies lie, and a judge has reviewed the issues with the parties. It is also usually after this appearance that the lawyers have a good grip on who they are dealing with in their own client, in their opposing counsellor, and in the other party.

After the case conference, either party is at liberty to *bring a motion*, which is an appearance where a judge *is* permitted to make a substantive order or to decide the issues brought forward in the motion. Motions are expensive and sometimes have long waits associated with them. And they are not guarantees: asking a judge to give you something doesn't mean that they will. In fact, it could go entirely the other way. But you will still have the bill to contend with. Across Canada, the cost of preparing for and attending a motion ranges from $3,000 in New Brunswick to $15,000 in Ontario to $20,000 in Vancouver. For one day in court.

SETTLEMENT CONFERENCE

If you don't achieve a settlement at or shortly after the case conference, the next standard appearance is a *settlement conference*. There may be intervening motions as described above. As at the case conference, the judge will try — again — to engage the two of you in discussing settlement options. The judge's job is to encourage you to come to some agreement and stay out of the court system. They don't want you there.

TRIAL MANAGEMENT CONFERENCE

If you don't achieve a settlement after the settlement conference, next comes a *trial management conference*. As with the period between the case conference and settlement conference, there may be intervening motions. This means that there are still issues in dispute, even if others have been resolved, and that the parties are at an impasse as to how to settle them. Once again, a judge will try to encourage you to resolve the issues, but this appearance focuses mostly on planning for the inevitable when you can't agree: a trial.

TRIAL

At some point way, way after your trial management conference, you'll be placed on a list for a trial. Sometimes that's twelve or eighteen months, or more, away. In many parts of Canada, there is currently a two-year wait for a trial date. When faced with these kinds of timelines, it's important to examine where you had hoped to be a year or two from now. How much older will your kids be? What do you see them doing then? What do you see yourself doing? Weren't you hoping this process would be far behind you by that point?

In all its unwelcoming, drab glory, court is trying to deter you. And it tells you as much when it says, "Well, you didn't settle so ... see you next year, sometime."

What do you do until then? That part is really up to you.

I'm not saying you should give everything up and walk away (though some people do), but I am asking you to examine your current circumstances and your own mental health and well-being and consider whether you can go on this way for that much longer. Remind yourself that even if you're content to ride out the lengthy wait until your trial, you might lose. Even if you think you have a great case. And if you end up losing, a judge may then order you to pay the other party's legal costs, as well as your own. Always assess that risk with your lawyer if you go down that road.

I once assisted on a trial in a tiny courthouse in a suburb of Toronto. The trial was scheduled to take four days. The file had been one of our most active for going on three years. The parents, it was clear, absolutely hated each other. They hated each other so much that they didn't seem to mind seeing their two children suffer because of it. I liked to think that they *couldn't* see their children struggling because they were so caught up in their own mess, but it was obvious. They dragged their young children into the court process by having them interviewed in a process called a *views and preferences report,* in which they had to tell a complete stranger where they'd prefer to spend their time. Imagine being a child and being asked to do this. I can't imagine it, but I can imagine that I'd be terrified.

Even though the children had communicated their preferences, the parents still forged ahead to a trial, as if to say that the contents of the report they'd put their kids through (and paid thousands of dollars for) didn't mean anything to them. The trial was on precisely one issue, which is somewhat rare in family law cases: Dad wanted exactly equal time with the kids that Mom had. Mom refused, time and again, but with no reasonable explanation. She just wanted what she wanted.

By the time the trial started on day one, the clients had each spent about $250,000 ($500,000 total) preparing for the trial, plus the years leading up to this moment. Both of them entered the courtroom dressed like they had job interviews. Then the judge, who was older and had been brought in from another jurisdiction to hear the trial, sat down and said, "Well, I read your materials." He exhaled deeply before leaning toward the microphone. In the most anticlimactic of moments, he said, "My back really hurts today. I'm going to go have lunch. You are going to go in the hallway and come to some kind of agreement. We will reconvene at 2:00 p.m."

Both clients looked stunned. They were so ready. Everything they had done to this point was in preparation for this big event at court. They looked back and forth between the judge and their lawyers, who were also taken by surprise. And then the judge said, "If you come back without an agreement, I will put an order on your file that says that when your kids turn eighteen, the ten boxes' worth of this file will be delivered to them so that they can understand why there's no money left for them to go to university."

Damn, I thought. *This guy gets it.*

The clients were absolutely taken aback. No matter how many times we had told our client how risky this process was going to be, he'd been adamant it was the right choice. He was certain that his former spouse would be read the riot act and made to look stupid in front of the court.

They left court with a deal later that day. Neither of them won.

So even at this late, late stage, resolution is still possible. Even at this stage, it is okay to weigh the pros and cons of continuing down this road. I see it happen all the time. In fact, in my twenty-year-long career, I have assisted in five trials. Just five. Out of hundreds of files.

Of those five trials, two settled on the eve of the first day of the trial. Another settled on the first day of a four-day trial. The other two went ahead. They went *alllll the way*. One trial lasted fourteen days, which, in the family law realm, is unbelievable, and I don't want to talk about it. I still have a twitch in my eye because of the number of all-nighters I pulled for that one.

And the worst part? Our team worked our asses off. And we lost. On every single point. The judge didn't like our client, and sometimes that's all it takes.

I'm telling you, stay away from court. It's a gamble.

Overview of Courts Across Canada

It is important to note that the laws and legal definitions in different provinces and territories in Canada vary, sometimes dramatically. Family law has always contained — and will always contain — a lot of grey areas, and this is yet another reason why having a strong team and a competent lawyer is so important.

The law is relatively clear on many points, both federally and provincially, when it comes to legally married couples. For whatever reason, whether you own that piece of paper or not has become the point on which many things turn, notwithstanding the nature, length, and significance of your relationship.

One of my favourite examples of the differences among provinces and territories is the definition of what constitutes a common-law marriage or relationship. Some definitions actually require (discriminatorily) that the parties not only live together for a prescribed period of time but *also* have a child together. Here's a breakdown by province and territory. Alberta's is the most mystifying of them all, and Yukon's is the most straightforward, though still confusing.

PROVINCE/ TERRITORY	Definition of Common-Law Relationship
Alberta	The term used is *adult interdependent partnership*. You must cohabit in a relationship of interdependence for at least three years, or in a relationship of some permanence if there is a child. You can also become an adult interdependent partner by entering into a written adult interdependent partner agreement.
British Columbia	You must cohabit for two years in a marriage-like relationship.
Manitoba	You must cohabit for three years, or for one year if you have a child together.
New Brunswick	You must cohabit continuously in a family relationship for three years, and one person must be substantially dependent on the other for support, or you must live together for one year and have a child together.
Newfoundland and Labrador	You must cohabit for one year and have a child together.

Northwest Territories	You must cohabit for at least two years, or have cohabited in a relationship of some permanence and together be the natural or adoptive parents of a child.
Nova Scotia	You must cohabit for two years.
Nunavut	You must cohabit for two years or cohabit for a period of some permanence, with your child.
Ontario	You must cohabit for three years, or have a child and a relationship of some permanence.
Prince Edward Island	You must cohabit for at least two years, or have cohabited in a relationship of some permanence and together be the natural or adoptive parents of a child.
Quebec	Common-law partners are known as *de facto partners*. Many laws in Quebec explicitly apply to de facto partners, similarly to spouses. Currently there is no clear timeline for becoming de facto partners.
Saskatchewan	You must cohabit continuously for a period of not less than twenty-four months.
Yukon	You must cohabit in a relationship of some permanence.

Family law and the courts across the country vary dramatically as to process, available resources, and the burden of responsibility that they place on litigants. This is in no way a comprehensive guide, but it is meant to give you more insight into how complicated the court system is so that you try your best to stay away from it.

In Manitoba and New Brunswick, for instance, people who commence court actions involving the care of children are required, as a first step, to take a six-hour-long parenting course. They have to actively participate and obtain a certificate before they are permitted to continue in the court process. I love this idea, and I wish that larger provinces like Ontario and Quebec had similar programs in place. In Toronto, future litigants have to attend a mandatory information program and their attendance has to be certified by a court clerk in order to proceed through the court system. The information program introduces parties to the alternatives to court and promotes alternative dispute resolution (that is, settlement out of court).

In British Columbia, the third largest province and very busy in the family law realm, there are no unified family courts. This means that if you go to court, your family law matter may well be placed on the same docket with corporate and commercial law matters and motor vehicle accidents. It also means that, in all likelihood, the judge hearing your sensitive family law case will not actually have family law experience, another example of the implicit risks of going to court.

Quebec, the second largest province by population, is the only province in Canada that operates with a civil code, meaning it does not use a common-law system and has never acknowledged common-law unions; instead, it refers to those types of partners as *de facto partners*. De facto partners, like common-law spouses in Ontario, have no rights related to property upon the breakdown of a relationship, whereas married spouses automatically have those rights. On that point, Ontario and Quebec are aligned with Prince Edward Island, Nova Scotia (sort of), Newfoundland and Labrador, Yukon, and Northwest Territories. However, British Columbia, Alberta, Nova Scotia (sort of), Saskatchewan, and Manitoba offer the same protection in terms of property division for married spouses and for unmarried, or common-law, spouses.

The above is just a smattering of some of the more obvious differences among the provinces and territories. I hope it highlights the importance of starting out with the right information. If you're going through a separation in Ontario, it's fine to talk to your friend in Alberta about it, but not fine to take their advice about, for example, how property is divided.

Because what applies to your friend in Alberta doesn't apply to you in Ontario.

We know now that children do best when both (or all) of their parents play a meaningful role in their lives. We also know that most (if not all) parents have unique things to contribute to their children's lives.

It's taken me a long time to accept that conclusion. My relationship with my father has been very strained since adolescence for a variety of reasons. Still, as hard as it is to admit, some of the things I like the most about myself are because of him: I am kind of funny sometimes, I have an excellent memory for useless information, and I would give someone the shirt off my back, the way he did.

I apply the same principles when coping with the estrangement from my dad as I do when I think about my son's father: I try to remember all the good and endearing things because it hurts a lot less that way. It doesn't negate everything terrible, but when I get stuck in the mud myself, it helps to dampen things a bit.

When I was in grade 2 or 3, I was learning how to tell time from an analog clock on the wall in school. When my dad came home at the end of his workday, I explained to him that I was working on telling time. His immediate reaction was to run, rum and Coke in hand, to find a tennis ball and a flashlight.

He took me out into our backyard in the darkness of the night to explain to me how time works. The tennis ball was the Earth, and the flashlight the sun.

Of course, this was entirely too complicated and not at all what I was expected to be learning. I am thirty-nine now and I can only tell the time on a digital device (thank goodness there are so many).

Every time I look at a clock face and ponder the mysteries of those hands moving around, I think of my dad, how hard he tried at that moment, and how capable he must have felt to dive into Carl Sagan territory. And I remember that everything wasn't always so bad, but that we never had the tools — either of us — to make it better.

When I think about my dad and how hard he didn't try, I remind myself that sometimes he did. If we had had better tools ... I don't know. The dad-daughter sky might have been the limit.

5

It Could Happen to You: What You Need to Know About Outcomes

WHAT IS THE WORST THING YOUR EX WOULD SAY ABOUT YOU?

I wonder how either of my parents would have answered this question, if either had ever seen the inside of a lawyer's office before their kids were already adults.

I bet my mom would say my dad cheated on her and drank too much. I bet my dad would say my mom ruined his life. Throughout my childhood I certainly heard those insults flung across rooms to rest at the feet of the other person like a grenade about to detonate. There was consistently a tremendous level of conflict, with my parents often yelling, "Just wait till the kids are older!" in front of us, as though they were doing us a favour by staying together.

The truth is, by the time my parents consulted with legal counsel, the damage to my sister and me was long done. To this day, nearly twenty years later, I live with many impacts from my exposure to their conflict. Some of the symptoms around food and exercise choices surface daily; like many children from high-conflict homes, as you'll read more about below, I struggled with an eating disorder for a long time. It was something I could control when I could control nothing else.

My parents separated when I was twenty. But at twenty, I was already doing this law clerk job and living independently. My dear little sister, on the other hand, was thirteen, at an entirely different stage.

Moving Ontario Family Law Forward Act

Custody matters in Ontario used to be guided by the tender years doctrine: an actual law that placed young children exclusively in the care of their "mothers." For no good reason. It all but ignored the other parent.

In November 2020, the aptly named *Moving Ontario Family Law Forward Act* received royal assent. It was proclaimed into law on March 1, 2021. The impact of this small act is massive: it replaces the possessive, ugly language we used for a painfully long time in the *Divorce Act, Family Law Act, Children's Law Reform Act,* and *Courts of Justice Act* with more neutral language. Today, we're governed by the *maximum contact rule,* the (sometimes harsh) reality that children should have as much contact with each parent as is consistent with the best interests of the child. The caveat is that the parent who is most likely to facilitate contact with the other parent should have the *decision-making responsibility* (formerly referred to as custodial rights) for the child. Child-focused terms like *parenting time* and *decision-making responsibility,* in place of *custody* and *access,* contribute less to the arsenal of those people and parents who choose to be adversarial. And we are seeing it work.

The new act also established a broad, almost all-encompassing definition of *family violence.* Specifically, and to the relief of domestic violence survivors, the act states that violence "need not constitute a criminal offence," acknowledging that when the abuse goes unreported it does not mean the abuse did not happen.

While the impact on me was mostly psychological, and while I am still working through the aftershocks of a childhood steeped in parental conflict, the effects on my sister's young life were palpable and life altering. Recognizing that my parents played a role in this, even unwittingly, has caused me a lot of grief. Did these people really care about us? Or were they so entrenched in their own issues that they didn't have the capacity to worry about us too?

Family law refers to evidence that is rooted in the social sciences and in the expertise about residential schedules for children. These days, family law promotes equal, shared parenting time so that children have an opportunity to spend just as much time with one parent as with the other.

Along with equal time, family law promotes jointly making decisions that affect children's welfare, where possible. This is often an exercise in extreme patience for parents, but it's an important one: when the children grow up and become young adults and then fully grown adults, they will appreciate their exposure to parents who came together, co-operatively, to make decisions about their schooling, health, activities, or whatever needs they had. They will remember that sense of togetherness, even when their parents were otherwise apart, and they will feel that they were valued and important enough to bring everyone — their two homes — together.

What family law isn't always great at is warning people of the possible consequences if they *don't* behave in a child-focused way. I have seen judges, obviously frustrated with parents who can't work things out on their own, warn them only vaguely about what could happen to their kids. And we've all seen the television show or read the book or watched the movie about the person whose life was blown wide open by their parents' divorce. While the possible outcomes for kids definitely exist along a spectrum, contingent on how their parents handle the most difficult circumstances post-separation, things can turn out very, very badly.

As a now-divorced, successful co-parent to my own children, I cannot imagine placing them in harm's way, figuratively or literally. I have a lot of insight — I see outcomes that other people don't see every day in their lines of work. Now that I am both a co-parent *and* a non-lawyer family law professional, a lot of people come to me to ask the same questions: What do I do? Are my kids going to be okay? How do I do any of this?

Yes, emphatically, they will be okay. But, also emphatically, this is utterly contingent on *how you and your former spouse conduct yourselves now*. The only truth about parenting post-separation is that you make your own luck. You are not lucky to be a good co-parent; you are working extremely hard.

Post-separation, you do not have a year (or three or five) to have your come-to-Jesus moment and finally decide that less conflict is easier. By then, the damage to your kids will have been done. If the root of parenting is putting your children first, your time to shine as a parent is during the separation and the period following.

Your children need you, their other parent, and an easy transition as much as they need oxygen and water. In many ways, how your children emerge from your separation is in your hands. And your hands only.

■

In my interviews with current co-parents and with adults who are children of divorce, the hardest part was their retelling of past trauma, particularly hearing that it was still very much in the present for many of them. During many of the interviews, I wiped my tears off the keyboard as I frantically took notes. That parents could have a hand in such terrible outcomes for their own children is the single most upsetting thing. As I have aged into adulthood and parenting myself, it is something I worry about every day.

Advice from Co-Parents

I know a lot about co-parenting because I've been watching people do it for twenty years and I've been doing it myself for five years. That doesn't make me an expert, in any way. But first-hand experience is relatable. When I first separated from my husband, I scoured websites, online bookstores, and self-help sections for books about separation and co-parenting, but I couldn't find what I wanted. I didn't want to read about how to emerge as some kind of "boss babe" with a great side hustle. I didn't want to read any book with a religious bent or by doctors or lawyers or psychologists who have never been divorced or who have not co-parented. I definitely didn't want to read about how I was going to get my groove back. The books that I did try, I didn't like or never finished.

What I wanted was the midthirties, moderately successful, professional parents' guide to navigating divorce without losing your shirt, your mind, or your cool. I wanted to know if it was possible to come out of this the way my family wanted: happy.

I made do with talking to friends, but even that had a low yield. I was the first to divorce in my group of friends, just as I had been one of the first to have a baby. There were times when my friends and I couldn't connect, and during my divorce was one of them.

My interviews with co-parents for this project were some of the funniest, most relatable experiences I have had. And some of the interviews — the ones where co-parenting wasn't successful — were some of the hardest.

One memorable interview was with co-parent Natalie — an entrepreneur in Toronto. Her daughter, Sara, was just four years old when Natalie and her husband split. Natalie admits that in the beginning, there was a lot of animosity. Her ex was hurt that the relationship had ended and that she had been the one to end it. When they first split, he did not want to engage whatsoever with her.

But Natalie knew what she wanted: a good, strong co-parenting relationship for the benefit of their daughter. So, she says, "I killed him with kindness." She elaborates: "I would send him photos of our daughter on a special occasion or doing a fun thing for school. I would send them and expect absolutely nothing in return, which is usually what I got." She pauses and takes a satisfied breath. "But I kept fighting for the co-parenting relationship I wanted, and I eventually got it. It was exhausting, but it paid off.

"I kept sending the photos, and then I started sending texts," she says. "The invitations to dance recitals, dinners, birthday parties, and other things that I thought Sara would appreciate having *both* of her parents present for," and "eventually he came around." His repartnering played a big part in that. Natalie says he was just happier and nicer to her, and that changed their dynamic considerably.

These days the two text daily, and Sara, now ten, has her own Sara's Family WhatsApp group, where her two sets of parents talk about her, share photos of her, and update one another about soccer games and school events and report cards. The four parents are a team now, with the common objective of raising a great and healthy kid. Natalie's persistence has paid off.

In the earliest days post-separation, Natalie says, "I wanted things that were unattainable or unreasonable — more of Sara's time, more decision-making abilities, or whatever other thing." Now, she says, "I don't really know why I wanted those things anymore.

"It was actually my own mother," she says, "who sat me down in the thick of things, on the verge of actually going to court, and said, 'Look, I know it feels like a huge thing right now and that it must be hard to imagine, but time moves so quickly and this won't matter in a few years.'" That was hard but absolutely necessary to hear, and it paved the way for the mostly harmonious relationship Sara's parents have today. When neither parent feels threatened and they both feel protected, the kids will, too.

Natalie adds this important advice: "Co-parenting and progress are not linear. There are setbacks, as there were in our marriage, for example, but the difference is that now we work through them. We talk. And we keep Sara's best interests at the top of the list."

Another great co-parent, Lisa, a single, cisgender, Ashkenazi Jewish woman and mom of two says it best: "When separating, you still need to remember what your job is as a parent." When friends who are embarking on their own divorces ask whether their kids will be okay, she replies, "Yes, but it will only happen if you don't talk shit about each other." She reminds us that "kids aren't stupid," saying flatly, "If you speak negatively of the other parent, or react negatively around them, the kids will come to their own understanding. They will carry that understanding through their stages of development. And, most terrifying, use the things they saw — good and bad — as guides in their own relationships."

She tells me about a recent day when her daughter asked whether or not her mom and dad were best friends. Lisa paused, thought about the best way to put it, and then said, "No, but we're really good friends and we love you both so much."

Wrapping your children up in love and support seems so corny when you're a self-admitted pessimist with daddy issues. But I think back to my childhood years, locking myself and my baby sister in a closet to muffle the sounds of the arguments happening downstairs. Feeling loved or cared for or, for that matter, like we were even there at all would have gone an inexplicably long way.

Nadine is a separated mom of two teenagers, who were nine and twelve when she separated. A hilarious co-parent, Nadine offers insightful advice now that she is on the other side of one of her life's biggest upheavals. "Be age-appropriately honest with your kids at every turn," she says. When her son specifically asked what was wrong, as the parents were carefully crafting the separation announcement in the background, she replied, "You're right that the energy in the house is weird. Dad and I are working through something, but we're not ready to talk about it yet." When I ask why her reaction wasn't to hide that something was wrong until it was time to talk, she says, "I didn't want my son to learn not to trust his instincts when he asked me if something was wrong. I didn't want him to grow up thinking his gut was wrong." That, my friends, is putting your children first. Even when you're knee-deep in grief. Even when you have no idea whether everything will actually be okay.

Susan self-identifies as a cisgender, bisexual, divorced mom of two. Her perspective, not always heard, is important. "If you can't produce children at home with your own at-home equipment and genitals, the state becomes involved," she says. "There are places where there's value in that and there are places where that's a real double-standard." Untangling her family dynamics and creating new ones has been an ongoing process requiring a few iterations.

While the family has now found some rhythm in co-parenting, "the kids are sixteen and twenty-one now, and hindsight is interesting." She says, "If I could go back and do it differently, I would have pushed for family therapy way earlier. We did do it, but later, and it was helpful, but I wish we had done it sooner." As Susan became aware of the importance of modelling, that children learn by observing their parents and their dynamics, she says, "I emphasized in my relationship now, and I told my partner, it's really important that you get up and wash the dishes — show them that for me — because they have seen unbalanced partnerships and I want them to see fairness and equality."

Susan left me with a valuable reminder to pass on to all parents embarking on creating a co-parenting dynamic: "Have some grace for yourself, too. This is also hard for you."

Charlotte describes herself as a mixed-race mom of two Black teen-agers, from Brampton, Ontario. She offers a poignant observation of co-parenting that I would be remiss not to include. Systems of oppression are everywhere, and they are ever-present in the legal system. They are engrained in governance, and we are slowly unlearning all manner of principles that have created systems that truly serve the needs of only a specific population: white people.

For Charlotte, co-parenting never felt like an active choice. It felt like the only possible outcome. "For my family," she says, "there was never the prospect of long legal battles or big lawyers' bills. We were young, broke people of colour with two little kids." Her children were eighteen months old and three and a half when she and her ex-husband split. They are thirteen and sixteen now. "We've grown up," she says, "and now we've known each other as exes far longer than we knew each other as spouses." Together, she and her ex celebrate holidays and kids' birthdays. They help each other out. He comes to her house to put up the tree at Christmas. The kids are surrounded by their parents' love and a strong example of what is possible when you take this path, whether by choice or force.

My inherent privilege as a cisgender, white woman means I view the legal system as just another place we can go when we need something. Charlotte, on the other hand, rightfully views it as something to be leery of, that doesn't represent her interests as a woman of colour or the interests of her Black teenagers. For her, the endgame wasn't how much money she would have or where she would live — but she doesn't intend to com-municate to people, especially to women, not to pursue that to which they are entitled. She says, "My endgame was to protect my mental health and my children's mental health. You can deal with the money and all the things later, but you can't do that if you drive yourself off a cliff. What's the point in fighting over a house if I'm not there to live in it?"

For Dean, a trans man and father of two children, one of whom he birthed, the legal system was similarly terrifying as a tool for aiding in a family law dispute. Dean says he and his former spouse wanted the best outcome for their kids, no matter what. But he also knew that — inten-tionally or not — the legal system was light years away from treating a family like his with the grace and empathy it is owed. "The issues are just different for us," he says. "Everything is just a little bit harder, a lot slower, and we are constantly explaining ourselves and our roles."

In the end, Dean and his spouse hired a mediator recommended to them by friends who are also members of the LGBTQ2S+ community. They then arrived at a most creative arrangement: they took out a small loan to renovate their semi-detached home into two separate units. Dean lives downstairs and his spouse lives in the apartment upstairs. The kids didn't leave their home, and Dean and his spouse get to parent the way they always intended, mostly. "We know this isn't conventional," Dean says. "But we aren't conventional. We also know we love our kids and that the sacrifices we've made have given them the opportunities to continue to thrive." Dean and his spouse took control of their futures, acknowledging that there would be time to heal once they were able to dig out of the mess created by a separation.

"We love each other still, very deeply," he says of his spouse. "She was there before my transition and she's here now. You cannot undo that kind of history when you share it with another person. There is no one in the world I would rather be separated from and parenting with."

Nicholas, a dad of two daughters in Toronto, offers this about his relationship with his eldest daughter's mom: "I was too afraid to ask for what I really wanted. I felt guilt and shame for bringing about the end of the relationship, so I just gave everything I had left." For years, Nicholas's time with his daughter was nominal: three or four overnights out of every fourteen. The rest of the time he missed her terribly and worried if anything could be done. "I knew I wouldn't be able to afford to fight in court about time with her," he says. "I also knew that asking for more time would be refused, from experience. I just hoped, with each passing year, that her mom would just come around and recognize that I was a good dad, and that my daughter and I had a great relationship."

And while that did happen for Nicholas, it was only many years later. When you think of the moments we have with our children and the memories we create, Nicholas's perspective on missing out is illuminating. "I've only gotten to be the tooth fairy twice," he says through tears. Nicholas's own childhood was greatly impacted by the loss of his dad when he was young. "I learned to hide the way I felt about things really early on, for the benefit of people around me. When I was offered the opportunity, as an eleven-year-old boy, to talk to someone — maybe a therapist? I don't really know — about it, I obviously turned it down. I wish someone would have been there to make sure I got the support I needed, because these things have a ripple effect. You carry them with you much longer than you expect."

American author and activist Glennon Doyle gives the example of being a passenger on a plane. Your flight has turbulence and you do what we all do when our minds shift abruptly from inflight entertainment to *OMG WE ARE GOING TO DIE*: You look to the flight attendants. Do they look relaxed? Does it look like anything unusual is happening? If they look stressed, you panic, but if they're still serving peanuts, you feel like everything is okay. When parenting through a separation or divorce, your job is to weather the storm, regroup, smile, serve the peanuts. It feels like the most child-focused recipe I've ever read.

My favourite co-parenting tip, as both a child of divorce and a co-parent myself, is this: when your children inevitably ask those strange origin-story questions or come home with family tree assignments (ugh), it's lovely to share an example of a time when their parents really loved each other.

My now-eight-year-old asked me, not long ago, if I love his dad. "Of course I do," I said. "He's your dad, and we're a family."

He nodded and went back to Minecraft. Worried I had oversimplified, I said, "Why do you ask?" His expression turned pensive. I was prepared for an onslaught of beyond-his-years questions, but he looked at me point-blank and said, "Can I have a snack now?"

Smile and serve the peanuts. Or, in this case, nut-free prepackaged treats.

Advice from Adult Children of Divorce

These were some of the hardest interviews I conducted. Adult children who hail from high-conflict divorces make for really interesting parents. On the one hand, they seem willing to do every single thing to make their relationships work, even to their detriment. On the other, conflict is often all they know. And it is a cycle that is repeated in their own lives.

Among all the folks with divorced parents that I spoke to, the most common sentiments related to the ways in which their adulthood was impacted. Many of these people spent their entire childhood without ever seeing their parents in the same room. Imagine that! Tournaments, graduations, recitals, birthday parties, and a parent who *could* reasonably be there is perpetually missing instead.

Then those kids became adults and had weddings and other events where they really wanted their family present. I'm sorry to say that for a lot of them (myself included), the parents could not find it in themselves to come together for a few hours to make their children happy or to celebrate their children's happiness. For those whose parents did agree to attend at the same time and in the same place, the adult kids spent the entire day panicking. *What if something terrible happens? What if my parents fight in front of everyone?* The same chorus of *what if, what if, what if* that they'd lived with as children and young adults.

One adult child of divorce I interviewed offers really insightful advice. Elizabeth is a cisgender, white mother of two in Toronto. "My own parents split up when I was eighteen months old, so I can't say I really remember that part at all. But then they both remarried and things were good for a while. And then my dad and stepmother split up when I was eleven, and my mom and stepdad split up when I was thirteen. That was when everything blew up."

Imagine how difficult it is just being eleven or thirteen, without the added and unusual stress of *both* sets of your parents separating.

"My parents went to court when I was sixteen," she says, "and they wanted to involve me in the process. It was ridiculous." Still, the impact has been significant. "I'm thirty-seven now and my parents have never really been in the same room at the same time. They both attended our wedding and one birthday party for one of our daughters. At both of those events, my focus shifted from what mattered — getting married and celebrating my daughter — to worrying about them getting into some huge blowout in front of everybody and ruining everything. I was embarrassed for them that it had come to that, that their adult daughter couldn't enjoy her own wedding or a birthday party because of their never-ending conflict."

Her best advice to separating parents is this: "Do everything you can to do what's right for you in your life — set boundaries, listen to your gut, trust yourself." And "when it comes to your kids, remember why you married, or partnered with, the other parent in the first place. Think about the moments where you started to plan a family or even think about one and thought that the other person would make a good parent. Believe that those things can still be true, just different."

In Elizabeth's case, a little awareness on the part of either of her parents would have gone a tremendously long way. As an adult, she says, "I'm working on it every single day. Not to let old patterns creep in."

Thinking of her own young family — a four-year-old and an eighteen-month-old — she says, "While your kids are young and in your care, *you* are the thing that makes them feel safe or not safe. That sense of safety will surround them for the rest of their lives. The feeling of security is cellular: it imprints on them." She pauses to take a break before she reacts to bad behaviour or poor listening or some other typical parenting irritant. You can't undo a lot of things, but you can do so, so much better than the examples set for you.

I wholeheartedly agree.

Alexandra, a partnered mom of three and an entrepreneur, relays important, if painful, advice. "My parents' dynamic and the impact on me and my siblings taught me what *not* to do in my own parenting life."

That's a sad but common sentiment from a lot of kids like us.

"When my parents separated, it was like my dad was just … gone," she says. "He started another family with his new wife, and my brother and I became these weird outsiders." This was about thirty years ago, so their mother had sole custody and the parenting schedule meant that they spent so little time with their dad that their relationships with him, compared to what he has with his two other children, were just not as important and never the same.

"The modelling I saw," she says, "showed me a lot of things that didn't feel right or seem right and so I avoided those things. But I'm lucky. And I've made some mistakes along the way and learned a lot from those, too."

No matter which route you take to settle your issues, Alexandra says it's really important to put the adults in their place. "Parents choose separation, *not* kids. The kids should never feel as though they've lost anything in the process. They shouldn't even really know that it's happening, where possible."

There are countless examples of the long-term impacts of poor parenting (or, I guess, a lack of focus on the kids during the separation and afterward) that should give you pause. Stephanie, a mom of one, says, "After my parents split up it was like I lost my dad completely." Stephanie was adopted as a baby, adding a layer of trauma to an already complicated dynamic. Her relationship with her dad developed such a deep rift that years later, when she hesitantly called to invite him to her wedding, he said, "Save the stamp."

Likewise, Leah, a single woman and accounting professional, has been deeply wounded by her parents' dynamic. She is forty, but she still feels the way she did as a child. "I wish I had discovered therapy sooner," she says. "It has helped a lot, but I have lost so much time, too."

Time is a thief, but conflict is the greatest criminal.

> Because of what I do for work and the ages of my friends and acquaintances relative to divorce rates, I get asked often — really often — for recommendations for lawyers, often with the caveat that they be aggressive, or something along those lines.
>
> After pausing to reflect on how grateful I am for my own experiences and years of work, I say, "I know a few, but I'd never recommend them to you." When they seem shocked or disappointed, I explain further. "It's just that I don't think that's what you need. I think you need someone thoughtful, considerate, and child-focused. *Aggressive* isn't one of the words I would use to describe any of my favourite lawyers."
>
> It always takes them a second, but then they, too, pause for a moment. "Yeah," they say. "You're probably right. So … who would you hire?"

6

It Could Happen to Them: What Outcomes for Kids May Look Like

I CONDUCTED MANY INTERVIEWS WITH FAMILY LAW LAWYERS, mediators, psychologists, social workers, school guidance counsellors, and pediatricians. I received so much excellent information that I couldn't fit it all into this book. What I took note of was this: unanimously, they warned of ominous, disturbing outcomes for kids who are exposed to high levels of conflict.

Advice from Lawyers

Lawyers offer a very interesting perspective on parenting, especially when they've been practising for many years. Those who have been around at least as long as I have in the family law realm have seen the profession through many overhauls in a short period of time, and I have witnessed them uphold the evolving spirit of the law in a way that makes me proud to work with them.

My interviews with lawyers have brought me great comfort, because despite the diversity in the focus of their practices, their general personalities, their province of practice, and — in the case of the lawyer from Montreal — a completely separate legal system, they were all mostly aligned in believing that, in most cases, children should spend as much time with both of their parents as possible. And that parents should stay away from court.

You may be interested to know that all eighteen lawyers I interviewed had, like me, only worked in family law. It seems ridiculous to say that it's a calling. They all wanted to be lawyers, of course, but they also wanted to help *people*. Not corporations or insurance companies.

When I warmed to the idea of being a law clerk midway through my college program, I had already dreamt of a million ways I might be able to use these newfound skills to help people or to be kind or to make small change. Sometimes, helping people doesn't have to happen on the grandest of scales. Sometimes, making small changes in the life of a real human being and their family is invaluable. I still hear from clients whose files haven't been active for a decade. Their lives have changed and evolved so much since I worked with them, and they are kind enough to still tell me how grateful they were for the support they received way back when and to update me on what they're doing — and how their kids are doing — now.

When I asked the lawyers about the harsher language that federal legislation used before the amendments to the Divorce Act — *custody* (now *decision-making responsibility*) and *access* (now *parenting time*) — many admitted that they had been using the softer language for quite some time. Personally, I always found the older words to be highly negatively charged. Imagine being the parent who ended up spending less time with their children and being referred to in court documents as the *access parent*.

One of my favourite family lawyers, Lorna Yates, hasn't used those terms in a decade or so. "I quickly learned to codify my language when I recognized that the use of words like *custody* made a parent feel like they were on the bad side and not the good side of something." She says, "I very much bought into the process of both parents having strong roles, and of consistently using more family-friendly language, despite having been mentored at a time when family law was very different."

I work for her, so I have seen this approach in action and have loved watching its successes.

When the lawyers I interviewed were asked how they would handle new clients who come into a consultation absolutely hell-bent on having sole custody (now referred to as sole or joint decision-making), they were unanimous in their responses. As a starting point, Adam Black, another of my favourite lawyers in Toronto, says that "parents need to recognize that each parent is different and able to offer something meaningful and important to the children's lives." In most cases, each parent having equal importance in the lives of their children and "seeing things through the lens of that being integral to the success of our children now, later, and much later, is vitally important."

Adam hails from his own separated parent dynamic but with a fresh and unique perspective. He became involved in family law, in large part, because of his experience following his parents' divorce and their subsequent remarriages. In his case, he says, "I moved through childhood and into adulthood with a deep and genuine sense of gratitude for the bigger, better, more loving family I ended up with, all of whom are still close knit." He acknowledges that while there may have been some conflict initially, it subsided and is not what he remembers most about his upbringing. This perspective "was what I wanted to take to a separating or divorcing individual, with the hope of being a catalyst for creating different results."

I ask what his best advice would be to, say, a friend who approaches him about their own separation involving young kids. He says, "I would tell it to them straight. Children do better when both of their parents are meaningfully and positively engaged in their lives. And that people need to, *early on*, reframe their often knee-jerk reactions to things. Perceiving everything to be conflict laden when it's probably just a poorly written email is dangerous."

When I ask Lorna Yates, who is a parent to young children, for her best advice to a friend going through a divorce or separation, she offers the simple but effective "People who know better do better." I gasp when she says this. Sometimes the most profound is the simplest.

About putting clients on the right path, Ms. Yates says, "I am in love with the idea of keeping lawyers *out* of negotiating parenting time schedules." Instead, when young children are involved, she encourages people in the earliest stages to go to a parenting mediator. While this may not suit everyone's needs, it has proven to suit most people's and to be more child-focused and cost-effective than having the lawyers negotiate back and forth.

Brigitte, an experienced family law lawyer in Montreal, is clear and firm in her observations. "Clients come in for consultations, and to temper what I anticipate their expectations to be, I tell them that they are here for a consult and to be informed of their rights and recourses, with the objective of reviewing all of their options in light of the circumstances. This means that, at times, I may have to tell them something that they will not want to hear. But this is an important aspect of practising family law. Parents need to make informed decisions, since they may have a long-lasting impact."

"As an attorney," she says, "we have a duty and responsibility to strongly advocate for alternative means of resolving conflicts between parents. Evidently, one of the options when parents are in a highly conflictual situation is going to court." But she is very clear as to what the court system entails and the adversarial process that parents are plunged into and must navigate. "When they insist on going to court, I tell them: If you go down this path, it's going to be costly, difficult, and emotionally taxing. And, at the end of this journey, you may not obtain your objective or your goal, since the person who ultimately will be making the decision as to custody or parenting time with your children is neither you nor your partner/spouse but a third party, a judge." Her objective is to "get families out of the courtroom, if possible, since neither parents nor children want to have a judgment imposed upon them." The "win-lose perspective of the judicial system unfortunately fuels conflict."

Brigitte has her own unique family dynamic. She and her separated spouse continued to do many family things together, in the interest of the children. Driving together to out-of-province hockey tournaments, participating in school activities, and attending all sporting events. Married or not, she had very strong feelings about the importance of parental presence in the lives of her children. "We may no longer have a marital relationship, however, in the eyes of our children, we are their parents and will always be. As a result, I strongly believe that our children benefitted from our ability as parents to communicate with one another and to be available for them in whatever capacity that was needed of us at the time. As I often say, when it comes to your children's happiness and well-being, you find a way to buy the peace." Her kids are grown now, and she has really fond memories of their childhood because of the approach taken.

Jack Haller, a married father to two teenage boys in Moncton, New Brunswick, whose wife is also a lawyer, says the most interesting shift he's seen in family law — the exact time of which he cannot pinpoint — "was when the onus fell to 'Mom' to explain why equal, shared parenting *doesn't work*." Indeed, it used to be much easier — implied, even — that the kids would just end up with Mom. The world is a different (and hopefully better) place now, and this has changed in a relatively short period of time.

Another of my favourite lawyers, Deborah Graham, now practises collaborative family law (see chapter 3) and mediation exclusively, meaning she will never go to court again for a client or take on a litigation file. She is also a pre-eminent instructor to newer lawyers and those embarking on careers in mediation. She teaches mediation training and also instructs lawyers and mediators how to screen for domestic violence and power imbalances.

When it comes to knowing your clients and their needs and to identifying the signs of intimate partner violence and domestic violence, Graham has what is likely the most effective tool I have heard of. She starts her multiday mediation training with a meditation.

Not just any meditation, she says. "I walk students through the morning, twenty-five years earlier, when I drove to work listening to the news on the radio. Without naming names, the news told of a small town in Ontario where a woman and her four children had been murdered. I knew. And then my phone rang. My assistant was calling to tell me that the police were at my office waiting to speak to me; it was the woman I had just met with a week earlier. The one who said she was scared, but she didn't know why."

She says that for her unsuspecting students, her story takes domestic violence screening from a box they need to check off as part of their training to something they desperately want to know more about. They ask how she knew it was the woman who had consulted her and what was she thinking when she heard the news?

"For me, that moment many years earlier became the basis for my own brand of trauma-informed service." She says that "just like changing the language as it relates to family law from *custody* to *decision-making* and *access* to *parenting time*, shifting language is so valuable and important in so many ways. The way we have seen humans extend humanity to one another when *What is wrong with you?* is changed to *What happened to you?* is a really powerful thing."

Understanding why people feel hurt and why they may, in turn, react a certain way to a certain trigger is key to unlocking the mysteries of how people behave when they are engaged in family law matters.

Advice from Doctors

A warning: this section contains sensitive information about self-harm, disordered eating, and abuse of children.

Lawrence Pinsky, an experienced and decorated family lawyer in Manitoba, points out the statistic that of all the children who are the product of a high-conflict divorce or separation, the social science, which is not as robust as one might hope, indicates that approximately 90 percent will suffer negative experiences; but despite the sometimes-hellish environments they encounter, they still come out okay. Only approximately 10 percent end up faring really poorly. The question that must then be asked, apart from trying to prevent or minimize those terrible experiences, is what are the predictors of those poor outcomes? What puts a child in that 10 percent? Might there be pre-morbidity issues or family of origin, and/or temperament issues? "The ship hasn't sailed" in terms of a definitive answer, Mr. Pinsky says. "There's still a lot to learn." For the time being, in my opinion, it makes sense to consider that an approximate 10 percent risk of a very negative but preventable long-term outcome is too high for comfort when thinking about your kids.

Dr. Cara Davidson, a consulting pediatrician based in Ontario, reflects on her years of practice working exclusively with kids. She deals with the 10 percent that Mr. Pinsky refers to, but it's a full-time, round-the-clock job. "Parents often come in seeking — even begging — some kind of diagnosis for their child. I can understand that," she says. "I have kids of my own and I understand wanting answers." Running her own practice and working out of the hospital, she is exposed to children in all manner of situations, some emergent and some ongoing. Children in crisis are, unfortunately, nothing new to her.

When we speak about children in the midst of their parents' conflict, Dr. Davidson says resolutely, "I wish I could just take one of my prescription pads and write, *Mom and Dad, just get along, please*, on it. It really could be that easy. We make it hard."

"Generally," she says with very little reservation, "at the clinical level, I can tell when the parents are problematic and a barrier to the child's success and well-being." She says that "we are all equipped with the parenting skills we have based on our own lives and the parents we had. That can be good and it can be bad." She acknowledges that those skills often fall short of what the kid standing before you needs. From there, it is necessary to do something — anything — to improve the situation, whether that be counselling, parenting resources, or any number of other tools.

She believes that parents often want a diagnosis to explain their children's "maladaptive behaviour" (often presenting as conflict, stress, or anxiety) because, as she puts it, "it is much easier to put a label on something than it is to change the way you parent." *Maladaptive behaviour* is a big phrase that runs the gamut from anger, withdrawal, avoidance, passive aggression, and emotional dysregulation (inability to control emotions or having big emotional responses) to poor performance in school or a refusal to go to school at all.

She likes to put the focus on her patients by asking them direct questions. "I ask kids what they think would make things better for them." Each time that she hears "I wish my mom and dad wouldn't argue," she says "it hurts, because I know in many cases, by the time that a child has been able to formulate those thoughts and feelings and to verbalize them to me, a stranger, a lot of damage is already done." Indeed, with a wait list eighteen months long, by the time she sees these kids, they have already been living this way for too long.

Among the more serious outcomes Dr. Davidson sees are eating disorders so severe that admittance to a hospital becomes necessary to support the child. She recalls treating a patient for many years who lived in an extremely high-conflict home. Her patient became more and more ill year after year and was admitted to hospital multiple times for treatment, and many years of self-harm brought about her death as a very young woman.

"Her body was just too weak to pull through," Dr. Davidson explains. "Eating disorders are so common because diet and exercise are one of the only things young people feel like they can control when it feels like everything else is so hard." It should not be overlooked that anorexia and bulimia do not end at controlling your own behaviours: they are mental illnesses. Anorexia is considered the deadliest; more people die from anorexia or by suicide with anorexia than die with bipolar disorder, depression, or schizophrenia. Eating disorders include anorexia, bulimia, binge-eating disorder (which often doesn't meet the clinical criteria for diagnosis but can also be severe with long-term impacts), and overeating. While eating disorders are thought to predominantly impact females, 25 percent of males will encounter an eating disorder in their lifetime.

She says these types of outcomes are all too common in children and teens from high-conflict situations. Although some of them, somehow, go on to do well in their lives, the majority do not. Trauma is trauma and it impacts each person, and each brain, a bit differently. "A parent should never rely on the rare case of a child doing well despite their own terrible behaviour as a guide," she says.

Among the other outcomes Dr. Davidson sees is post-traumatic stress disorder in infants caused by exposure to certain dynamics in their homes. She sees, and makes, frequent diagnoses of attention deficit disorder and attention deficit hyperactivity disorder, for which patients are often medicated and managed with other forms of treatment. "There is a chronicity to these things that parents can't see when they are actively behaving in ways that they shouldn't be." She says, "I wish that I could hold a mirror up to them showing them the future if they don't stop what they're doing now." Sometimes, she says, "I have to look at parents and say it is never okay to expose your child to harm. You wouldn't push them out into the road in front of a car, so why would you do this to them?"

To add insult to injury, says Dr. Michaels, a pediatrician in New Brunswick, that province encounters statistically higher levels of domestic violence and intimate partner violence than many other provinces. "There is a lot of poverty in New Brunswick," he says, "and sometimes these things come hand in hand." Dr. Michaels is a general pediatrician with a special interest in providing gender-reaffirming care to young people. Often, he says, "once a child makes their way to me, there is already a lot of trauma."

Dr. Michaels is called upon frequently to testify in court as an expert in custody disputes, where the court is effectively asking him to comment on the appropriateness of one parent's having custody over the other, based on his observations. "I try not to choose one over the other, except in cases of physical violence," he says. "I refer parents to all sorts of parenting resources, government programs, and I have a library of books I offer them to keep for themselves. We all have a lot to learn and I truly believe that most parents want to be good parents, but they don't always know how to do that." He is a big fan "of giving parents chances to improve without turning the child into some kind of guinea pig."

Dr. Michaels keeps tabs on his patients and their families, knocks on doors, and makes sure people are doing well. He brings patients in to see him, checks on their school progress, and looks into other indicators of health far outside of physical health. "If there's something bad going on," he says, "I will see it." His hope is that for parents in New Brunswick, many with limited opportunities and their own histories of trauma, a new wave of parenting can be created. "Everyone is capable of being a good parent but we are only as good as our support system."

That says a lot if you don't have a support system at all.

The outcomes for the 10 percent of children from high-conflict homes who do not fare well (an under-researched area of social science) also include short- and long-term drug and alcohol use problems, poor performance in school with devastating impacts to the child's educational future, inability to foster friendships and relationships, and criminal behaviours (theft, for example, is seen with some frequency in kids from high-conflict homes). And the list goes on.

Of course, not every child who hails from a high-conflict home will meet this fate. But that's not an insurance policy, and it shouldn't dissuade you from starting off on the right foot — now — and making sure you never have to look back and wish you had done things differently.

One parent I interviewed talked a lot about the things he regretted, and there were many. From the start, he regretted not pursuing what he wanted and what he thought was best for his daughter. He regretted feeling so remorseful about ending his relationship with his wife that he chose not to rock the boat. He regretted trying to remain diplomatic while simultaneously feeling so much guilt that, in the end, he felt he lost too much time with his kid.

Although I sometimes think you can never have it all, I think you can in many ways. You do not need to feel guilty for the choices you make in your life if they ultimately bring you the ending or new beginning that you want. Guilt, like time, is a thief, and kids grow up quickly. You don't have to have a perfect relationship with your ex in order to have a good co-parenting relationship. These things can improve over time if you work on them — just like anything.

7

When Things Aren't Easy: Parenting Coordination, Voice of the Child, and Dispute Resolution

WHAT IS THE WORST THING YOUR EX WOULD SAY ABOUT YOU?

One client responded, "I put myself before the kids, routinely." As we navigated a process with that client, it became evident that was absolutely true.

We cannot change people, and people don't often change much from what you know them to be. It's important to remember that, to digest it and make it a part of your approach to everything. I have wanted to take former partners by the shoulders and shake literal sense into them, but it's not actually possible. People do leave certain family law processes either empowered or enlightened or beleaguered, and they definitely learn a lot, but to say they leave a *changed* person is overreaching. They will inevitably return to their usual behaviours, and some people will need to be kept in check.

A very experienced family law lawyer, mediator, arbitrator, and parenting coordinator in Toronto, Seema Jain, says it best. Think about it this way: your child might sit on a couch one day and complain about you to a therapist. Of course, that could happen no matter what, but it's far more likely if you forget who you're here for.

As I have said, co-parenting doesn't come naturally to everyone, and in rare cases it doesn't work for everyone, either. If you're one of the people reading this with an impossible-seeming ex, I promise that I'm well-acquainted with all of the possible outcomes.

Sometimes the adults are stuck in the weeds and can't find their way out. Sometimes the parents know only conflict (sometimes, generationally), and they don't know how to do hard things any other way. That's not necessarily their fault, but they need to invest in working through it for the benefit of their kids.

Parenting Coordinator

When your relationship dynamic with your former spouse presents with more conflict than you can handle, but you are still embarking on co-parenting, your lawyer or a judge might recommend engaging a *parenting coordinator* (often referred to as a PC). PCs are lesser-known but invaluable players in family law. Most often, a PC is a family law lawyer or a social worker who is trained to de-escalate conflict when working with parents through strategies and education. Like one of my favourite lawyers said, when we know better, we do better. We don't all come into parenting as experts (or even close), and many of us carry a ton of baggage, the you'd-have-to-pay-overage-fees kind of baggage.

Parenting coordination is used frequently in Ontario and is gaining traction in other provinces, with more and more professionals offering it as a service.

The sole focus of a PC is to ensure ease in all things child-related and to keep the parents at bay. A PC can help the parties iron out big and small details in their parenting plan. In higher-conflict scenarios, a PC can become a sort of enforcer of the separation agreement, parenting plan, and even court orders. PCs encourage respectful dialogue and solutions around issues that come up. They may referee two grown adults who can't seem to make a decision without someone watching them. Whatever the reason you might need one, a PC is a really effective tool.

Most often, parties will agree to retain a PC for a prescribed amount of time (often two years, but the days are long and the years are short) and the PC will work directly with the family to ensure that both parents know their agreements inside and out, know what's expected of them, and know what they need to do. When a dispute arises, instead of fighting with each other or running to their lawyers, the parties take the issue to the PC. The PC either enforces the agreements and tells the parties to adhere to them or helps them to achieve a one-off solution, if that is what's needed. Let's say you're in a dynamic where the residential schedule for pick-ups and drop-offs has to be adhered to right down to the minute. (By the way, leaving zero room for human error is erroneous in itself; flexibility is key.) Let's then say that your sister is getting married next month and your kids are the flower children, but this is supposed to be the kids' weekend with their dad. In a reasonable world, you'd say, "Hey, your former sister-in-law, who you love and respect, is getting married this weekend, and I know it's the kids' weekend with you, but they are involved in the wedding, and it would be really unfortunate if they couldn't attend. Is that all right with you?" In some worlds, for God knows what reason, the other person will say no. They will dig their heels in, they will uphold the sanctity of the agreement because this is their goddamn weekend. And then the kids will watch TV all day instead of going to the family function where they would have had a wonderful time, seen their extended family, and celebrated in positive life events.

I have seen kids kept from participating in great things simply to adhere to the residential schedule, just to hurt the other parent. Was it in the best interests of the kids to miss these great things? Probably not. Will the parent who refused to be flexible likely need a favour one day in the future? Absolutely.

When issues like this arise and the parties cannot co-operate, a PC can break the impasse. They are reasonable, child-focused professionals who will help broker a deal. Maybe there will be a limit on how long the kids can stay at the wedding, or you'll have to leave early to take them home, or something. It'll never be perfect, but it'll be better than a flat-out no.

Parenting coordination can be costly, and the costs are typically shared by the parents since both benefit from the services. But for many families, it's an excellent investment that actually saves money by providing the conditions that avoid going back to court.

The Voice of the Child

The United Nations Convention on the Rights of the Child declared in 1989 that children have the right to be heard at every step in family law proceedings. While this is inherently an excellent development, it raises many questions and can be misused.

At what age does a child have a right to be heard? Well, it is widely accepted that the age of twelve years represents a sort of magic number, when children cross an invisible threshold from being protected in the background to being at the forefront, with things to say that adults are required to hear. We saw the age of twelve become a magic number in some Canadian provinces and some of the United States during the Covid-19 pandemic when the Pfizer Covid-19 vaccine was approved for children twelve years old and older. Suddenly, children of twelve did not require parental consent to obtain a vaccine; they could walk into a pharmacy or doctor's office alone and of their own volition and direct a pharmacist or medical practitioner to vaccinate them.

VIEWS AND PREFERENCES REPORT

A views and preferences report — which is conducted by an experienced family law lawyer, mental health professional, psychologist, or social worker — imparts to the reader (the parents, their lawyers, a mediator, a judge, etc.) what the child has expressed as their wishes — effectively, where they want to spend their time and how. The body of the report sets out what the child says they want, ranging from where they wish to sleep at night and who they want with them at doctors' appointments to how often they wish to speak to their parents.

These reports are most often used for children twelve and up, because that age represents a benchmark under various other acts of legislation. In addition, many professionals who prepare these reports won't consider interviewing children younger than twelve. In certain limited circumstances, the views of younger children may be given if they are siblings of a child twelve or older.

A views and preferences report can be useful when the parents cannot agree to a residential schedule or when the child wishes to express their opinion (or one or both of their parents think it should be expressed).

You can imagine the many ways in which this principle can be bent and twisted to suit the needs of parents with agendas.

The need for a views and preferences report can arise when each parent is saying something different about what their kids want or when the parents don't agree on major issues. It may also be needed when the parents don't share values, such as when one parent has a strong parenting ethos or religious affiliation they feel the children can benefit from but the other parent disagrees. In other words, there is an impasse.

The general rule of thumb is that a child never wants to hurt a parent's feelings or say anything bad about them. They're kids, and they just want everyone to be happy. Sometimes, in negotiations or in court, one party will allege that the child wants X and the other will allege that the child wants Y. In family law, there's truth and there's proof. We can tell the truth until we're blue in the face, but proving our allegations is important. For some folks, that necessitates having this type of report prepared.

If parents want to get a views and preferences report, it must be either ordered by the court or agreed upon by the parents as the next step. Either way, choosing the right practitioner is important. This person, like your lawyer, will have a significant amount of influence.

The practitioner, once chosen, will often start by explaining the possible implications of the report to the parents and to the child (in an age-appropriate way). The outcomes may be shocking to them. The practitioner is, in many ways, assessing the parents' readiness for whatever outcome they're heading for. Parents may push for steps like this when they believe they are right beyond measure. But just as when parties are preparing to set foot in a courtroom, this type of high-level conversation is sometimes necessary to understand the gravity of what they have gotten themselves, and their kids, into.

The practitioner will explain to the parents that they might hear something in the report much different from what they'd expected — that phenomenon of the child's telling each parent what they think the parent wants to hear so they won't hurt anyone's feelings. This emotionally heavy risk gives pause to many parents, and once they have a better understanding of what's involved, some families find another way. But sometimes parents will still want to proceed with the report.

If you do proceed, the process is customized to meet the needs of your family. The person conducting the report will decide, based on the facts of the case, which steps to take. Often, they will meet with each of the parents separately before talking to the child. If the child has a therapist, they will speak to that person, too. If necessary, they will also assess the relevance of interviewing collateral witnesses, like the child's teacher, doctor, or other important figures in their life. Then they will meet with the child alone, without the influence of either parent.

Meeting with the child is, of course, the most significant part of this process. The person will never come out and say, "Hey, where do you want to live?" Instead, they'll have a conversation about the child's life, interests, extracurriculars, schooling, and friendships, and the information will, more often than not, flow organically. Some kids don't want to talk, and it's obvious that they don't want to be caught in this weird negative space between their parents, both of whom they love. The person conducting the report will note this, too.

Know that these reports, once tendered — no matter what they say — are most often strictly applied in court. This means that the judge will likely look at the report and say, "Well, this person is the expert, so we will rely on this report." These reports, good or bad, will inform the next many steps in whatever process you're in. The lawyers, the mediator, and the court will all rely on the contents. They will use the report as a guide for devising a schedule.

If you decide you don't like what the report says, you can't just make it disappear. The report will linger for many years to come, even when it is wildly outdated, even when the children are much older.

While I believe that reports like this absolutely have their place, as with many things child-related, they represent a moment crystallized in time. For a lot of families, that moment is taking place during their lowest point. Things are bad, really bad. Maybe the worst they've ever been. You've separated, you each think you know what's best for the kids, and you each think different things are best. You're both stuck in your positions, unwilling to see anything from another angle.

What I know about people knee-deep in grief is this: they are rarely at their best. They are struggling; their mental health is complicated; they feel a constant sense of impending doom. It's a painful way to exist, yet many of us end up caught in that cycle, languishing in the long delays between events in a family law case.

It's all about choice. A views and preferences process is somewhat invasive, it is time consuming, it is expensive, and it makes no guarantees. It may be the right decision for your family, but I believe that in most cases, with some very hard work the parents themselves can make decisions that meet the children's best interests — even when that doesn't look the way they expected it to — without the need for this type of intervention.

A quick word on misusing these reports: there are family law files that include allegations of *parental alienation* — this is an allegation by one parent against the other that their psychological treatment of the child, their influence and manipulation, has alienated the child from the other parent. A views and preferences report is a risk to families where *true* parental alienation has occurred, because, of course, it represents a very difficult time for that child. I say true alienation because an allegation of parental alienation is actually very serious, and a finding of parental alienation in a court is very challenging and rare.

CUSTODY AND ACCESS ASSESSMENT

When parents cannot agree on decision-making responsibility and residential schedules and when one parent believes that the other should be limited in what they can and cannot do as a parent, it may become necessary to undergo a custody and access assessment. In Ontario, this is a court-ordered assessment under Section 30 of the *Children's Law Reform Act*. It is conducted by an expert, a custody and access assessor who is typically also a psychologist or a social worker, and results in a report that sets out the needs of the child and the ability and willingness of each parent to meet those needs. Other provinces and territories have similar types of assessments prepared by someone appointed by the court.

Despite being court-ordered, a custody and access assessment is not usually court-funded, although some provinces do fund the cost of obtaining one. In most places, this process, which is just a small piece in a big family law puzzle, can cost $10,000 to $15,000 or more, and the parents usually split the cost.

And then there's the invasiveness: the assessment usually involves an interview with both parents, at least one interview with the child, and observational visits with the child in the care of each parent. If necessary, an assessor will also view any documents or reports germane to the facts of the case, such as report cards, medical records, police reports, and so on, and will conduct collateral interviews with people such as the child's teacher, daycare provider, doctor, therapist, and grandparents, as well as the partner of either parent.

The report typically takes a few months to complete, and then copies are provided to the parents. And the wait lists to get a report are long. Not many professionals offer this service.

Here are my comments on these types of assessments:

First, I have never had a file where either parent was completely satisfied with the contents of the report. Imagine a person looking at your parenting under a figurative microscope and then reporting it to someone who gets to make major decisions about your life.

Second, these reports represent just a snapshot in the life of a family, likely not at its highest point. They can be provocative and compelling, and they eventually become woven into the narrative of future court proceedings or negotiations.

Third, while judges usually rely on these reports, they don't have to. They will still decide the fate of the family before them, and they are not bound by the terms of the reports.

What you want to consider before embarking on a custody and access assessment are mostly things of a practical nature:

- Do you really need a report? Is there another way?
- Do you think that the results of the report will reasonably but dramatically tip the scales in either your direction or the other parent's?
- Is a report cost prohibitive for your family?
- Are you comfortable with having your kids intimately involved in a court process?
- Have you tried everything else there is to try?

As with every topic we explore here, undergoing a process like a custody and access assessment or a views and preferences report is not an experience we ever expect to have. These processes are heavy, expensive, time consuming, and full of emotional labour.

Keep an ongoing dialogue with your chosen team of support people about the necessity of something like this. Remember that you and your ex are both human beings, and short of physical violence or other forms of abuse, you're probably both good parents. Is there another way? Even when this feels like the only way out, discuss the options and revisit the things you have likely previously discussed with your team. You may find that you have a little left to give and can find a way that will benefit everyone.

Future Disputes and How to Solve Them

In my non-lawyer opinion, a separation agreement and a parenting plan are only as strong as their dispute resolution clauses. That is to say, all agreements should have in place a detailed, secure *dispute resolution mechanism*, or a section called *dispute resolution*. The section should clearly and concisely set out exactly what will happen should one (or both) parents take issue with a part of the separation agreement or parenting plan, which — spoiler alert — happens with some frequency and is one of the reasons I have a job.

Agreements that do not have dispute resolution provisions or have really limited ones are, in my opinion, a failure on the part of the lawyers who prepared them. Leaving clients out in the cold should a dispute arise is effectively ensuring repeat business. And that's not in the spirit of family law, in my view. We are meant to give people lasting solutions.

One of the parents I interviewed, for example, has one of the weirdest separation agreements I have seen (and I have seen many). Absolutely limiting and rigid, at every opportunity it diminishes the role of one parent over the other. He and his ex share a child, and the ex had sole custody (now called *sole decision-making*) and the majority of the parenting time. In fact, from the beginning of the separation and for many years after, he had only about three out of every fourteen overnights with his young daughter. You can imagine the impact this type of schedule can have on a child's relationship with their parents. You can imagine what it would be like to see your child so little and the impact this would have on your mental health over time. This is precisely the kind of thing we never think of when we start a family and have kids. And it is absolutely heartbreaking for the parent who feels they have "lost."

Plan to Fail

A good dispute resolution mechanism gives the parties a predictable road map of how to get from the first declaration of a problem with one of the terms in agreement to a solution. Most dispute resolution sections provide the following steps:

1. You need to notify the other party, in writing, about the item you have an issue with. Say, for example, that you want the location of a transition (a change in care from one parent to the other) to change from the school to the swimming pool. Propose a solution. The other party has a specified number of days to respond to you.

2. The two of you should try to negotiate a resolution. Chances are you're still paying off the line of credit you took out for your original tranche of legal fees, so see if you can just figure it out yourselves.

3. If you've tried hard but you just can't negotiate, you go to mediation (described in chapter 3). A good dispute resolution section will suggest mediation. A great dispute resolution section will name the agreed-upon mediator in advance. A really great dispute resolution section will name the agreed-upon alternate mediator should the first one not be available.

4. If mediation hasn't helped, you may need to pursue mediation-arbitration. Most dispute resolution mechanisms either end at the assumption that a decision will be reached in mediation, or go further, committing the parties to mediation-arbitration if they are unable to achieve a resolution in mediation.

5. If you cannot come to an agreement through mediation, and you did not already agree to proceed to arbitration, then the dark side sets in. Your very last option is to take your issue to court and ask a judge to sort it out.

In this separation agreement, there was a very limited dispute resolution section. It simply stated that the parties should try to negotiate a solution themselves or through their representatives. And it literally ended there. Like an escalator ascending to nowhere.

As the non-custodial parent, often referred to as the access parent, this meant, realistically, that he could approach the other parent, who could then simply say no. If he had the stomach for it, he could hire a lawyer and likely end up in court, at the cost of many tens of thousands of dollars. And maybe, after all of that, nothing would change, even though this parent describes his daughter as hesitating to leave after their short amount of time together or, when she got older, actually saying that she wanted to spend more time with him.

Family law is very much a choose-your-own-adventure kind of thing. Court is not an adventure, though, unless you count all the trips you'll make to the bank and all the sleepless nights. Having a path *already* forged for future disputes that may (or may not) arise is like having home or car insurance — it is a safeguard.

My former spouse and I had a strict no-video-game rule for our boys back when we had, maybe naively, set out their futures in our heads. We never played video games growing up, and we didn't want our kids playing them, either. It was just one of those parenting ideals, like organic produce or hemp clothing or attachment parenting. Ideally, we wanted our boys to be reading Dostoevsky and to, like, wax philosophical at an astonishingly young age, or to learn the right phrasing so they could recite a Shakespeare soliloquy as a party trick for all the entertaining we never ended up doing. But we didn't want them running around with pixelated swords and shooting at things.

And that was totally fine, until I repartnered with someone who brought a great many things to my life and my boys' lives, including game consoles. He had put himself through school playing video games professionally and had an intricate understanding of video games that far exceeded my knowledge of them.

My younger son was immediately attracted to the consoles. Many of his young friends were already playing video games, and he felt the urgency of a kid who feels left out. He wanted to play, and he wanted to play a lot.

In the end, my former partner and I sorted it out: our son plays video games in one house and not in the other, and it works just fine. We went with the flow, within reason, and we stay in touch about it.

8

Ecosystems: Making One Family in Two Homes

WHAT IS THE WORST THING YOUR EX WOULD SAY ABOUT YOU?

I once dreamt that my ex would respond, "All she ate were pastries. Never meals."

The "one family, two homes" idea has been around for a long time, and it is reality for many families. When you have, indeed, one family living in two separate homes, you begin to recognize the gaps between your homes, and you may find the need to revisit certain ideas with your co-parent.

Both homes and parents should always try to present a united front. Undoubtedly there will be one "fun parent" and one who isn't so fun — if you're being real with yourself, you know which one you are. That doesn't mean you need to quit your job, shave the side of your head, and start serving cookies for breakfast to appear cooler (no judgment if you've tried this). And it also doesn't mean you need to start reading books about appropriate discipline for children. It just means that this is yet another place where you need to give a little and take a little. Or maybe a lot. I happen to be the fun parent and the one who occasionally serves cookies for breakfast. But the truly important things — like expectations around school work, reading, and extra-curriculars and the way we validate feelings, talk about our days, and discipline and reward our kids — we do together and we do similarly.

There may be different activities in each home — my ex is legitimately obsessed with basketball, and I stopped loving it after the five hundredth game. Again, each parent brings unique things to their kids' lives.

You are a sort of ecosystem for your children. A kid's ecosystem is meant to be both their safe haven and their happy place. It should be an impenetrable force field of good judgment and priorities that are in order. The kid's ecosystem is a shared space. It connects both households and, if parents are repartnered, two families in infinite ways.

You will share the joy of raising your kids, but you'll also share many things that do not spark joy, like disgusting illnesses that come home from school. When this happens, it suddenly feels like your parenting plan has been thrown out the window, but like life, it's really just a matter of adjusting.

Children are adaptable.

Say it with me now: *Children are adaptable.*

In fact, they are so much more adaptable than we are because they are young and have the advantage of neuroplasticity. We fail to acknowledge this fact much of the time, which is why we end up putting so much pressure on ourselves, as separating parents, to do certain things in certain ways, to our detriment, instead of appreciating that we have done this hard work to ensure that the kids will actually be all right. In fact, they'll probably be happier because we are happier.

When it comes to adaptability in children, we also should be careful not to selfishly take advantage of that trait, whether intentionally or unintentionally. We should use it for their benefit.

Parenting plans and parenting provisions in separation agreements consider many scenarios. Effectively, you are agreeing to certain actions to insulate yourselves from future conflict. But circumstances will undoubtedly arise that you did not contemplate when negotiating those agreements because, well, it's hard to imagine tomorrow, let alone a few years from now.

Your kids' ecosystem is your family's bubble of safety. Events arise in a child's life that need game-time decisions. Others require two heads to work out the logistics.

When creating your agreements, it's important, as I've said, to work with someone who will point out eventualities that you might never think of. You can read Ontario's precedent separation agreement or the Association of Family and Conciliation Court's parenting plan precedent as guides (see chapter 12). You can also ask friends to show you the parenting provisions in their agreements. Seeing what these things look like on paper is really helpful, and it takes some of the mystery out of the process.

Below, I've set out some of the more contentious issues that we don't automatically think of when we think of separating. I offer these as food for thought, especially if you are choosing to prepare your own draft separation agreement.

Transitions

Transitions refer to where, when, and how the kids go from the care of one parent to the other. Many parents find it easiest to have the children's schools or daycares be the point of transition. If one parent drops them off at school and the other picks them up, there's a natural flow. Making transitions complicated adds stress to the already busy weeks of families.

It's helpful to be explicit in your parenting plan or separation agreement about where transitions will take place, both during the regular school year and on specific days like school professional activity days and holidays, when transitions would likely occur at the home of one parent or the other.

Kids do best when transitions are both minimized and simple. They also thrive on structure and routine. With transitions, predictability is key.

Mobility

Mobility refers to moving your residence and, therefore, your children's home with you. Written into my own separation agreement is the declaration that the boys' dad and I won't live more than ten kilometres apart now or in the future. This is one of those issues where the children's best interests need to prevail; spending much of their time with you in the back seat of your car in traffic is not ideal. While this may mean that you and their other parent pay incredibly high housing costs to stay close together (as in my case, sigh), it is, ultimately, lovely to be close together, for many reasons.

My kids often forget things, or there's a theme day at school that one of us forgot about but the other has the accoutrements for, or the kids have left their homework or need a raincoat. I live two kilometres from my boys' dad. I can walk there in twenty minutes. One day, the boys will be able to walk back and forth on their own with ease. We work as a team on Halloween: one of us takes our younger son out while the other stays home and hands out candy with our son who doesn't do well in crowds or costumes.

It's important to be explicit about distance limits between homes, while recognizing that future circumstances can change, and that things may happen that incite a need for one parent to move farther than they had ever planned. Indeed, I have assisted in court on motions where one parent suddenly wants to move fifty kilometres away from the other but still maintain the same residential schedule by leaving home at 5:00 a.m. (with the kids) to get them to school in the other parents' catchment. Ultimately, the kids' interests have to be the most important factor and the solutions need to focus on the children.

Putting everyone's needs before yours is the weird part of parenting that no one tells you about, but it is necessary. Making space for yourself and your own needs is also important, but the well-being of your children depends on your decisions (as it would if you weren't separated), and every decision needs to be made with them in mind, first.

Kids' Belongings

Written into most agreements is that kids can travel between homes with whatever belongings they want. It doesn't matter who bought the new doll or the track suit — the items belong to the child, not to the purchaser. Items from home give kids comfort. Plus they'll inevitably want to show you some of their things. It's lovely when your kids want to share their days with you because, suddenly, one day, they won't. Savour it. Think of the annoying people sipping their giant lattes on the playground who sigh and say, "The days are long; the years are short, huh?"

A fantastic co-parent I interviewed told me that a brown bag containing devices for school, umbrellas, and similar items travels between her kids' homes.

Items travelling between homes is okay. And if your child wants to have a photo of their other parent in their room, that's okay, too. It is such a huge step in adult development to move out of "me me me" territory and into a place where you can have a photo of your ex and your kid together in your home and not flinch. I know — I've done it.

Communication

The issue of communication is a big one. This refers to both communication between the parents about the kids and communication between one parent and the kids when they are with the other parent. Of course, in most family situations, communication between kids and their parents should never, ever be restricted. My kids speak to their dad multiple times per day when they are with me. I do, too. He gets regular updates about what they're doing, how their vocal lesson went, what length of bike ride they took. I get regular updates about Friday night dinners, hikes, and family outings.

We both always know what the kids are doing, the way we would if we still lived in the same home, and it's a really nice feeling. That's not to say that we'll need to do this forever, but at this stage, and at our kids' ages, we just do. That will change — one day we won't have nearly as much to communicate about. But for now, it's so nice to know what my kids are doing when I'm not with them. It gives a fluidity to time that is comforting.

In their agreements, many families will choose to specify times when kids can contact the other parent. I'm not a huge fan because, again, life knows no boundaries. Putting something into an agreement that you won't be able to adhere to is setting yourself up for failure. And that was never the idea.

Communication between parents is different. In cases where conflict can be anticipated, parameters are often set. Lots of parents agree to communicate by text or email only. Some specify when or how many times a day. Putting limitations on the unpredictable in life can be frustrating, can feel limiting, and can create a scenario where there is more animosity than there needs to be. Remember, life isn't restricted to Wednesday evenings between eight and eight fifteen.

Introducing Your Kids to a New Partner

When devising a parenting plan or separation agreement, if you and your co-parent agree, it may make sense to incorporate terms covering the introduction of your kids to new partners and their kids. And, in some cases, introducing your kids to the kids you had with your new partner while you were still with your old partner.

Every agreement should specify at least some parameters around re-partnering and how that will impact the kids. Timelines and rules provide some predictability and keep the kids safe from potential harm. Harm isn't always physical: a kid may get really attached to a parent's new partner, only to have them disappear in three months. Sometimes that's unavoidable. But sometimes it's clear the parent should have known that person better before trying to integrate them into the kid's life.

The standard that I see these days seems to be that people date and are blissful adults falling in love for a minimum of six months without worrying about introducing kids into the mix. Many people who are trying to be child-focused tend to wait a year before introducing their kids to a partner. But a lot of people get caught up in the big feelings of early love and introduce them earlier.

Mostly we wait because we want to be sure whether that person will stay once they see you in parent mode (if they don't, they weren't for you anyway), whether they'll like your kids, and — the really big one — whether your kids will like *them*.

Personally, I was worried that any potential partner would run for the hills after an introduction to my kids. Not because my kids were terrible, but because they were little, with little kid needs. I didn't have the same appeal, my inner light didn't shine as bright, let's say, when I was wiping snot off someone's face or helping them in the washroom. To be clear, I have always been very firm that being a parent is a big part of my identity, from Pinterest-fail birthday cakes to Valentine's treats to meticulously planned homemade Halloween costumes.

Once, I showed a guy I was dating some pictures on my phone of the best Halloween costumes I had made for my kids. Looking at those pictures and how little my kids were when I dressed them up like David Bowie or Elliott from *E.T.*, I got sentimental. The guy got really quiet, and I looked up at his puzzled face. He actually said, "Wow, you're, like, such a *mom*." Like an insult. Like *Wow, you're such an asshole*.

This, among many other reasons, is why you wait. Just get to know the person and make sure they know you. Make sure they know you are a parent (hopefully, a parent first) and that's not likely to change for a couple of decades.

You also wait because it just makes sense. I talk more about this in chapter 9, as well as about the ins and outs of introducing kids to new partners and to new partners' kids. And — take a deep breath — about what blended families can look like, eventually.

Illnesses

Children's illnesses are interesting to navigate in a co-parenting situation, especially on school days, whether the child wakes up sick and can't go to school or becomes sick while at school. Technically, *technically*, on a day when a transition is occurring, the child is the responsibility of the person whose home they came from until the end of the school day. But real life doesn't always work that way. I work ten minutes from the kids' schools. Their dad works about ninety minutes away. Who's the best person to scoop them up from school if they're sick? Unfortunately, probably me.

Again, it's about what's best for the kids. You'd never leave your sick kid waiting hours for you if you could avoid it.

When a kid wakes up sick, technically they should remain with the parent whose home they woke up in. But what if that parent has an important meeting they've been working on for weeks? Or a flight out of town for a work thing? Or no paid sick days? This is what I mean when I say that sometimes you have to make game-time decisions. You talk. You consult. You, maybe begrudgingly, get into gear and do what the situation and the kids require.

In my experience, if the atmosphere isn't one of flexibility and openness, many parents find it almost impossible to abide by the rigidity of their agreements. Many times I have written letters to counsel on the other side of a file, trying to enforce the strictest protocol because a parent was fifteen minutes late or forgot to send the kid to school with rain boots. It has never felt like the best use of a client's money, and it has never felt particularly much like real life. I have, many times, forgotten to send my kids to school with something, both in my married life and my divorced life.

When we were expecting our second son, Steve and I knew this would be our last kid; we'd planned for two.

We had gone all out naming the first child, giving him the most imposing of Old Testament names and a calmer middle name, which he could use if he grew to decide his first name was too heavy for the real world. With the second son, we had too many choices. I had a list of names on my phone: names in combination, names matched with his last name, and names I hadn't yet shared with Steve because they'd come to me in dreams or through the pages of books I was reading on my morning commute.

We landed on something — maybe Jackson. Or Jarvis? Or Andreas? And we were okay with that.

And then that kid came into the world late and like a hurricane. His delivery was quick and scary and painful. I was stuffed into a tiny delivery room and the air was charged with stress, but you'd never know that looking into his big grey baby eyes. He was the calmest thing I'd ever seen. He looked at me like he was contemplating my worthiness to be his parent (this has not changed, actually), and he was completely serene.

The name we'd chosen wasn't right. So we chose Rivers. One of the discarded first or middle names from a long-ago list. It wasn't what we had planned, but it suited him so well.

9

Altering Your Ecosystem: How to Talk to Your Kids About Things They Might Hate, Like Divorce and New Partners

A GREAT FRIEND OF MINE AND HIS SPOUSE WAITED UNTIL IT WAS obvious their two teenagers already knew before telling them that their twenty-five-year marriage was over. "I bawled my eyes out in front of them," he says. "I was so sad for them." His ex-wife turned to him — the woman he'd married when he was barely in his twenties, who had seen him through hairstyles, midlife crises, infertility, and horrible gift selection — and said, "Jesus, you didn't even cry when they were born." The kids, he says, burst out laughing while he sobbed uncontrollably, the years of anticipation of this very conversation having spilled over.

Talking to Your Kids About Your Separation

Depending on their ages, talking to your kids about your separation may be challenging, but it's necessary. Many families choose to work with a family therapist or another child-focused professional to determine how best to tell their kids about their separation and the inevitable changes it will bring. Some lawyers can also give great advice in this regard.

There is no right or wrong way to do this, as long as it is age-appropriate. And the timing is ultimately up to you.

Some families prefer to tell the children right away. If you've been living in conflict and if your kids are middle-school or high-school aged, it's possible they are already anticipating it — kids are really smart. If they're younger, it may come as an enormous shock, and they may have big feelings and lots of questions.

This will likely be one of the most difficult conversations you'll ever have with your kids. You may find it easier if you follow a few simple pointers:

DECIDE ON AN APPROACH, *TOGETHER*

Again, there is no right or wrong here. You may not yet have all the details about what is going to happen at this point, but if you do, you can share as much or as little with your kids as you feel is appropriate. Presenting a united front will offer the kids comfort and stability. It will illustrate that you are working from a solid foundation (even if it feels shaky) and that everything is going to be okay for them.

TELL THE KIDS, *TOGETHER*

Presenting a united front will also start off the co-parenting vibes the right way. In the most non-blaming way possible, tell your kids that you're separating. You don't need to use the word *divorce*, and many kids won't understand that anyway. Refer to yourselves, their parents, as *we*, still. We have made this decision. We have decided this is best. We want our arguments to stop, and we want to focus on keeping you kids healthy and happy. They don't need to know who decided to end the marriage. And they definitely don't need to know why. One day you might consider telling them, if you're comfortable (when they're like thirty-five, over a glass of wine), but today? Not the day.

The reasons you are splitting up aren't important to them — trust me on that one. But they need to know, inherently, that you will give them the support and reassurance they need and will continue to need through all the transitions that a separation imposes.

REASSURE YOUR KIDS THAT THIS IS NORMAL, *TOGETHER*

Don't assign blame. The young ones won't care; older ones will. Tell them that lots of families look the way their family will look. Give them examples of peers, friends, and family members who also live in separated families. Normalize divorce, as negative as that may sound, because it happens a lot.

If your older children press you for more information, you can say how hard you both tried to repair things, how much you still care for each other, how excited you are to raise your kids together but in two separate homes, and, most importantly, how much you *both* love and care for them.

TELL YOUR KIDS ABOUT THE CHANGES THAT ARE COMING, *TOGETHER*

Maybe you have already negotiated a residential schedule. Maybe they won't be able to walk between your homes. Maybe you'll live in different towns. Being prepared for transitions has a huge impact on how stressful we perceive the transitions to be. Walking your kids through what a typical week in their new lives will look like is a great idea, if you have a picture of what that might look like. If a lot of things are changing — particularly if neither of you will be staying in the family home — remind your kids of all the things that *are not* changing: same schools, same friends, same grandparents, same parents. Just happier and more relaxed.

TELL YOUR KIDS THEY ARE ALLOWED TO FEEL HOWEVER THEY WANT

There is no right or wrong response. They can be angry; they can be sad. They can assign blame, even if they don't know anything about the situation. They can be frustrated. Just like you, your children will undergo a grieving process. Their family, as they knew it, is changing.

STAY CALM WHEN YOU'RE TELLING THEM

This is big. Do not cry. Do not be buzzing and full of anxiety. Be calm and explain, even if you're anything but calm on the inside. They will receive the information more calmly than if you are bawling your eyes out.

If you are calm, they can focus on their own feelings instead of worrying about you. That's not their job.

KEEP THE LINES OF COMMUNICATION OPEN

Tell your kids that if they have questions, you can have another family talk, or they can talk openly to either parent. If the conversations happen separately, make sure to fill your co-parent in on what has taken place so everyone is on the same page. Invite the kids to talk to you any time they want. And when they inevitably drop the *Why did Dad leave?* bomb in the schoolyard during pickup, answer the question appropriately and carry on. Kids don't have many boundaries when it comes to discussions about sensitive topics, but they should also not be made to feel that they've done something wrong when they ask you a question.

KEEP THEM OUT OF YOUR LEGAL WOES

If your file ends up a messy one on the property or support front, keep the kids out of it and do every single thing you can to avoid it impacting your co-parenting relationship. Your children and the way they develop and learn to conduct themselves in relationships in the future are more important than the house you have to sell or the RRSPs you have to split or the furniture you need to divide. Way more important.

DON'T DISPARAGE THE OTHER PARENT, EVER

I realize that there are limited circumstances in which the other parent is a legitimately bad person. I've seen that. If that's the case, your kids will likely come to this conclusion on their own one day. But even bad people — I hate to say it — can parent effectively. Do not let your opinion of the other parent damage your children's relationship with them, or with you for that matter. Some of the lowest forms of adult behaviour I have seen in my twenty years in this field stem from parents' shit-talking each other. It's not cool. It might make you feel better about yourself for five seconds, but it will never make your kids feel better about themselves, and that's what should matter most.

GIVE YOUR KIDS ALL THE TIME THEY NEED TO GET USED TO THIS

It's a new season for them. There will be lots of adjustments and many new ropes to learn. Do not rush them to be cheerfully accepting of all these changes from the get-go. Putting that kind of pressure on a kid who isn't ready is a recipe for disaster.

CHECK IN WITH YOUR KIDS

Don't barrage them with text messages or leading questions, but do check in. Ask them how they are feeling about their new routine, their new homes, and life generally. If they have something to say, they'll tell you if they feel comfortable and protected enough to do so. If they do not feel safe, they won't talk to you, and that can have truly tragic implications for a family.

Remember that all good things take time. You're all in the midst of a transformation, and it's probably easier for you, either because you chose this or because you've had time to digest what is happening.

Remember, *even* if you do everything in the best way you can, it might still turn ugly for a time. Kids may get angry when they can't verbalize exactly how they're feeling, and they can suffer in turn. Their school performance may dip, their friendships may be impacted, and the level at which they interact with you might change for a while. That's normal. You've just flipped their life upside down, after all. They will still be okay. Keep reminding them that you both love them, you both care for them, and you care for each other. Remind them that you are still a family, just different from the family you used to be.

Introducing Your New Partner

Another thing we never imagine in our lives together is repartnering. Why would we? In fact, many of us enter into marriage happy to put the weird social experiment of dating behind us. I remember sitting across from Steve during a rare night out. The two people seated at the table beside us were very obviously on a first date and very obviously had met on a dating app. Steve and I cringed at some of their lines, and in that moment I felt closer to him than I had in a really long time. I reached for his hand and said, "Fuck, I'm so glad we never have to do that again." Little did I know.

Repartnering is full of mystery. We don't know who that other person will be, what will make them tick, or how many of their own kids they may come with.

As mentioned in chapter 8, one of the provisions you might not think about when you negotiate the terms of your parenting plan or separation agreement is how and when it is appropriate to introduce your kids to a new partner and, in some cases, that partner's kids. One of the kindest things we can do for our co-parent, and for our children, is to exercise patience and discretion. Don't get me wrong: I know the exciting feeling of a new relationship — I've been married three times. I remember when I was dying to introduce family or friends to the new person, but I tempered my excitement for a variety of reasons, which multiplied when I had two kids in tow.

Kids thrive on routine and consistency. The people in their lives are among the most constant fixtures for them. That's why we keep them in the same schools and send them to the same daycares, and why they tend to keep the same friend groups. So parachuting your new partner into the lives of your children requires careful planning and thoughtful consideration.

First, you'll have to acknowledge the relationship, which you've probably been quiet about to avoid hurting anyone's feelings. I remember when I first realized Steve was in another relationship. I had driven to his home right after a snowstorm to drop off the boys' snow pants, and a woman was standing at the end of my old driveway. I had no idea who she was, so I walked right past her, knocked on the door, handed Steve the snow pants, said goodbye, and returned to my car, walking past her again.

I put two and two together pretty quickly, and by the time I had fastened my seat belt Steve was at my car window. "Is everything okay?" he said.

"Sure," I blurted out, way too loud and unconvincingly friendly. Then I burst into tears.

Now, to be clear, I was in another relationship, too. Still, I had all sorts of feelings to choke on. What did this mean for our co-parenting relationship? We've all seen those movies where the wicked step-parent dive-bombs in and wreaks havoc. What did it mean for my kids? Had they already met her and not told me?

I cried my eyes out for about ninety seconds, ugly, Claire Danes in *Romeo + Juliet*, kind of crying. Steve watched me, awkwardly shifting his weight from one foot to the other outside my open car window. Then he said, "Um, so that's a girl I've been seeing."

I responded, "First of all, that is a woman! Second of all, *I don't care.*" (Remember, people do not change much; I am a prime example of this.) Then I drove away, crying all the way home.

I talked to the friends I had in my parent group chat about it later that day, trying to understand what had happened to me. They were unanimous: after you've spent many years with a person, loving them, living with them, making their lunch for work every day, and carefully folding their socks, it would be very unusual *not* to have an emotional response to this situation.

Ultimately, you and your co-parent decide the terms of how and when to introduce new partners to your kids. It's best that you agree on these in advance. That way, you will already have a plan in place when this emotional situation arises. You'll have done that work when much cooler heads prevailed and the idea of either of you having another partner was just an abstract concept far in the future. Those years, though, they move quickly.

As discussed in chapter 8, many agreements that do cover repartnering stipulate a one-year period, or at least six months, before children are introduced to the new partner. That may seem like a long time, but consider that if you have your children with you every other weekend, and thus can't be with your new partner on those days, by the time you're a year into the relationship, you've spent at most twenty-six weekends with that person. That is to say, you've not spent one whole year together. If a year seems like too long, you can agree on a term of at least six months. You may find that this never becomes an issue anyway. Plenty of people with kids are happy to take it slow and just enjoy the relationship before adding more people to the restaurant reservation.

As someone who has done this very thing, I have found it helpful to be open and honest with prospective new partners about my kids and my co-parenting situation. Some people will run for the hills, and if they do, they aren't right for you. Others will be genuinely curious about your kids. They'll see your role as a parent as something to be admired, not lamented. It helps to make it abundantly clear that your children come first, both by necessity and because they mean the world to you. The right person will appreciate these things about you. There may be folks who don't love your co-parenting relationship with your ex-spouse for all sorts of reasons. That will be something to consider if and when it comes up.

Here are some points to consider as you introduce a new partner and their children into your kids' lives or if your co-parent is doing that:

TAKE IT EASY

There should be an informal, casual tone to the first (or third or fourth) meeting with a new partner. The kids don't need to wear bowties or fancy dresses, and you don't need to go to a Michelin-starred restaurant (especially since the kids wouldn't eat anything and it would be such a waste). The person should not be introduced to the kids as your partner or girlfriend or boyfriend — in the beginning they should be introduced as a friend.

A lot of parents try to force these meetings because they're in love or at least enamoured with this new person. They want everything to be perfect. But when it comes to feelings, telling the kids to be nice or, even worse, that they *have to* like that person — telling them that they have to do anything in this bound-to-be-awkward situation — is a one-way ticket to a tense encounter.

I met my partner's daughter (the oldest of the four in our blended family) the day before her eighth birthday. Despite speaking separation agreements like a second language, I put a lot of pressure on myself to do everything right in this first meeting. We met in a group setting, with mutual friends and their kids. Group settings are excellent for these types of introductions. I was introduced as a friend. I had made her a carrot cake from scratch. I had also bought her a set of books that were my favourite when I was her age, but then I panicked that the gift would be overbearing, hid the books in my purse, and never told her dad. (So if you're reading this, surprise!) In these situations, you have to go with the flow.

The kids played and ate cake together, and we all went home to separate houses. And I stressed way more about it than he did.

His daughter was pretty indifferent toward me, and I her, for a while. I'm sorry if that makes me sound terrible. Relationships take time and effort and consistency. But not pushiness — pushing kids to do something they're not ready for, or comfortable with, is not consistency.

READ THE CUES

The kids will tell you, one way or another, how they feel about the new person. Let them be the guides in this process. If you need to take a step back, take a step back. The right person will be okay with this, even if they are a bit disappointed (that's okay, too).

It's hard to imagine your kids not liking this person as much as you do. You're in love! It's exciting! You want to know what the rest of your life is going to look like! *You like to plan.* But it's entirely possible that your kids may not fall for this person head over heels.

Talk to your kids. While they do not dictate who you can and cannot befriend, their opinions should matter and their feelings should be validated. Meeting new people can be hard, and it can feel threatening to your kid. They may wonder if you still love their other parent. They may wonder if you'll still love them.

Talking about feelings is so important, but it's something that many people are terrible at, especially if they've been taught not to. But it works: feeling validated provides a sense of security. Knowing that their feelings aren't wrong and feeling that they are being supported through a tough or transitory time breeds resiliency in young humans. I'll talk more about children and resilience in chapter 10.

BE OPEN WITH YOUR EX

It's best to be upfront with your ex about your new relationship so they're not blindsided when your kids mention the new person six months or a year down the road. Technically, it's none of your ex's business. But your kids are your mutual business, and anything that has the potential to impact them should be shared between the two of you.

BUILD IN ONE-ON-ONE TIME

If all goes well and you end up living with your new partner and possibly with their children, too, you will find it helpful to build in some time with your kids when this whole new family unit isn't present. Of course, the majority of your time will be spent together, because that's what families do, but working in some time to do something special with your own kids, together or individually, will remind your kids that they are your priority if things get intense on the family front.

Reassuring your kids that no one is ever going to replace either of their parents is often a good idea, too. In an age-appropriate way, do everything you can to ensure your kids that their family is not going to disappear; it's just going to get better and a bit bigger, and they're going to get so much love.

TALK ABOUT RULES FOR A NEW FAMILY

One weird benefit to repartnering and starting a family that includes your new partner and your own kids is that you get to — because you have to — have conversations you may never have had in your former life.

Talk to your kids and your new partner about schedules. Where will the kids be and when? Remember, the fact that you are living with a new person is *not* a good reason to incite a change to your kids' residential schedule.

Talk to your new partner about roles. What part do you want your new partner to play in your kids' lives? Do you want them to take on some parenting? Do you want them to be a trusted adult friend to your kids? Do you want them to be mostly hands-off? All of these things are okay — because they are your kids.

Talk to your new partner about finances; the division of household labour; expectations around parenting, presence, and discipline; and any other issues that have come up in your past life. Make sure you are on the same page, within reason (you'll never be completely on the same page all the time). Try to plan for those things to come up again. Plans are great.

Talk to your co-parent. What kind of role are they comfortable with your new partner playing? That doesn't mean they dictate the role, of course, but it's helpful to talk about it and to plan. You don't want to over-step any boundaries or have your co-parent feel they are being replaced. Conflicted feelings will inevitably surface — all of which are normal and okay. Again, these are probably conditions you never expected to be in. Talking honestly can help mitigate those feelings.

■

My favourite thing to say to my kids is that they're really lucky because they have four adults at home who truly love them and care about them.

Ultimately, there's no single way to be a family. It looks different for everyone. Some families live in one home. Some in two. Some people repartner but don't live together, especially if their kids are young. That takes a lot of patience and understanding, but it is possible. Some people repartner and create a new family in a new space.

All of these things are possible with careful planning and creative thinking. You will, in time, find the configuration that works best for your kids and, in turn, for you. You may try, and you may fail and need to redouble your efforts to work toward a new objective. That is okay.

At some point after our separation, my poultry-loving ex decided to become a vegetarian. I immediately got my back up and wanted to talk to him about it, to make sure he wasn't going to try to push his dietary ideals on the kids.

As I often do, I got a bit fired up as I drafted an email. I always put things in writing. And I never send the email right away. I sit on it. I ruminate a bit. More often than not the email never gets sent.

So I did the same with this one: I drafted and waited.

A few weeks later, my son came home and told me about digestive enzymes. I had had a particularly bad day, so I marched to my laptop, fingers ablaze, ready to send that note to Steve.

When I searched his name in my email window, an email exchange between us from many years earlier randomly popped up. I burst out laughing.

We had gotten married on Valentine's Day. (Cute, I know. Barf.) On our second anniversary he sent me the most beautiful bouquet of a dozen roses. They showed up at my desk, improving the ambience in my tiny windowless office by a million percent.

I am a sucker for a good card, so I went straight for it and carefully opened the tiny white envelope. The card, in a stranger's handwriting, read: JESUS LOVES YOU, AND SO DO I.

There was no name.

A mishap at the flower shop on their busiest day of the year. Steve is Jewish, which made it all the more hilarious. I kept the card for years.

I speak a lot about the value of reminding yourself that you used to (or maybe still do) love your co-parent. Moments like this help smooth the road through what can be bumpy times.

10

Taking Care of You and Yours: Protecting Your Mental Health and Your Kids', Too

WHAT IS THE WORST THING YOUR EX WOULD SAY ABOUT YOU?

A client once responded, "She was struggling with her mental health, and I was too selfish to acknowledge it until it was really bad. And then instead of supporting her, I ostracized her and made her feel inadequate as a parent and as a partner. I really, really regret it. I can't believe I said and did the things I said and did."

On an early date with my now-partner, Adrian, we had a decadent night out: fancy outfits, fancy restaurant, great wine, and tiny plates of strange food. We were having a conversation about things other than our kids or being parents — I think we were talking about our mutual un-realized dreams of farming on a small or large scale — when he stopped in the middle of a sentence and said, "I really miss Charlie today."

My heart sank.

My partner was a true "Wednesday dad" when we met. Over the years, I've become adept at identifying those parents who have ended up with less time than their former partners to spend with their kids. If you see them with their kids, you can tell. They always seem to be racing against a clock and making everything as fun and exciting as possible. Next time you're at a restaurant for dinner on a Wednesday night, look around. Of course, not every solo parent you'll see is a separated parent with less parenting time than their counterpart, but some will be.

This dad had good reason to miss his daughter: he had very limited time with her. He hadn't spent a Christmas morning with her in six years. His marriage to her mother had ended when she was not quite two years old, and he'd never gotten to play Santa in her memories. He truly felt that he was being made to pay for the mistakes in his marriage by missing these small but very big milestones. As a parent who had near-constant contact with her kids and co-parent, it was sad for me to witness.

Adrian showered his daughter with love when they were together. He deferred every meal choice, every decision about activities — everything — to her. He just wanted her to be happy, and he wanted their time together to be magical. And though limited in hours, their visits were idyllic. I have seen a great many parents, I know many parents, and I have three children of my own. Adrian was one of the best and his relationship with his daughter was full of ease and peaceful, quiet moments where they just understood one another.

When she wasn't there, which was the majority of the time, he missed her dearly. He wasn't really able to communicate with her when she wasn't with him, and he was worried to ask for anything more than what he had been permitted. So he quietly missed her to avoid conflict instead.

Many years have passed and their time together has increased significantly. Now that they spend nearly half their time together, it isn't all magic. But it is magical in the sense that it's a real life they get to spend together, without the clock ticking in the background the way it used to.

She's also twelve now, so there's a lot of twelve-year-old stuff. So that's fun, too.

I have watched her grow and, over the last few years, become more aware of what is happening around her. She started to ask questions, to identify the parenting dynamics present in the families of her friends, and to see the differences between other people's families and her own. It was around that time that her schedule changed and her voice was given some weight.

I am infinitely happy for the two of them, and I'm proud of her for using her voice to seek out what she wanted. But I'm sorry she ever had to. And I worry about the impacts on the mental health of children in her circumstances, who want to be heard but may never find their voices.

Your Kids' Mental Health

While preparing this book, I had the life-changing opportunity of interviewing Dr. Jean Clinton, a child psychologist who focuses on the impact of trauma on the developing (child) brain. Dr. Clinton refers to herself as a knowledge translator; she distills clinical evidence and dispenses it in what she refers to as "small doses" for regular people (non-psychiatrists and non-psychologists) to digest.

Over the twenty-year span of my career and the much shorter but still significant five years of my co-parenting life, the family law profession and the courts have become better acquainted with the importance of the mental health of both parents and children. We have seen, more and more, how outcomes — good and bad — are directly linked to the circumstances that existed between the parents both before and after separation. One thing I cannot stand hearing when it comes to kids and divorce is "It's okay! Kids are resilient!"

No, they're not. They're kids. And at their young age, they don't possess the skills to communicate how they are feeling in a way that makes sense to adults.

This is my unprofessional opinion: adults often use the concept of inherent resilience in children to excuse their own behaviour. Resilience isn't something that someone inherently has or does not have. We parents can foster resilience in our children. We can help them develop it, the way we help them learn to read.

The only thing just as important as *your* mental health is that of your children. Their mental health deserves support, too. There are tools to help us through those tumultuous times, but we need to be willing to use them.

I have read many parenting books and divorce books, as well as case law, legislation, and studies on divorce statistics in certain populations. None of it has been as compelling or evocative as the work of Dr. Clinton.

LOVE BUILDS BRAINS

Dr. Clinton says, simply, that love builds brains. It's the title of her book, in fact. She demystifies the science of psychiatry by translating scientific and clinical evidence for parents so that they can apply it to their own circumstances and give their kids the best chance possible for success in their new regimens.

Much of what Dr. Clinton says is not surprising. "Charlotte," she says to me, "relationships that are warm, responsive, and predictable help our children thrive. Relationships that generate intense stress can harm the developing brain."

Add that to the list of things I wish someone had told my parents. Sometimes I imagine child psychologists or therapists meeting with child clients and, like my former boss, posing an interesting opening question: What is the worst thing you could say about your parents?

ADVERSE CHILDHOOD EXPERIENCES

Adverse childhood experiences are important in understanding a wide array of outcomes in adults. The U.S. Centers for Disease Control and Kaiser Permanente conducted their original Adverse Childhood Experiences (ACE) Study between 1995 and 1997 with more than 17,000 participants from several demographics. The study looked at abuse and other adverse experiences in childhood and how they relate to health and well-being later in life. There were, of course, all sorts of findings. But the most significant, to me, was that more than 23 percent of participants reported parental divorce as an adverse experience. That is to say, nearly a quarter of the 17,000 participants endured a parental divorce that they found traumatizing.

The study divided adverse childhood experiences into three categories: abuse (all forms); neglect (both physical and emotional); and household dysfunction, which includes mental illness, an incarcerated relative, a mother treated violently, substance abuse, and divorce. Sometimes it's nice to give a name to something you've been living with for a really long time and didn't know could be characterized.

Among these categories, neglect was reported the least, by 10 to 15 percent of respondents. Reports of abuse ranged from 10 percent (emotional abuse) to nearly 29 percent (physical abuse). In the household dysfunction category, nearly 27 percent of respondents reported household substance abuse. Collectively, approximately 60 percent of respondents presented with at least one adverse childhood experience.

Looking at the health impacts, possible behavioural outcomes for people who have adverse childhood experiences include a lack of physical activity, and the resulting potential effects on their health; smoking; alcoholism; drug use; and absenteeism from work and school. From a physical and mental health perspective, possible outcomes include diabetes, struggles with body weight and body image, depression, suicide attempts and death by suicide, sexually transmitted infections, heart disease, cancer, stroke, chronic obstructive pulmonary disease, and broken bones. While there may be other factors involved in these outcomes as well, the study shows a strong relationship between exposure to adverse experiences in childhood and mental and physical health problems later in life.

Just as we need to remember that health includes mental health, it is extremely important to recognize that the safety of a child includes not only their physical safety, but also their less visible emotional safety.

TOXIC STRESS HARMS BRAINS

For children, Dr. Clinton defines *toxic stress* as the "chronic, severe, ever-present stress of poor parenting dynamics, fighting in the home, [and] fighting between parents," as well as stress from other sources including poverty, social circumstances, and parental mental illness.

Dr. Clinton gives us a lot to think about. She likens things we may not understand to things we do.

When we encounter a serious stressor, we enter fight-or-flight mode — all of us: babies, kids, teens, adults. Everyone. When an event is seen as a direct threat to our safety, such as being chased by a bear, the brain releases cortisol (the stress hormone) and adrenalin. The *stress response cycle* is activated, and we dive headfirst into fight-or-flight mode. As the threat is removed — maybe the bear sees another person it wants to eat more, so it leaves us alone — the brain releases acetylcholine, which moves the brain, and therefore the body, into a calm state. That's under ordinary circumstances.

If we experience chronic toxic stress, it's like the bear is chasing us day and night; that is, the risk is always present. In time, and it doesn't take long, the brain endures damage. We become irritable and our memory is poor. We have difficulty focusing and thinking critically, and we feel increased anxiety and fear. Now think about people you know who, as kids or teens, were living through bad situations at home or were being used as pawns in their parents' disputes. Think about how they behaved. See any similarities?

It used to be thought that the brain was sort of static. It was thought to have a fixed structure and a fixed number of brain cells, which were believed to decline over time with age and trauma. Now we know that the brain experiences *neuroplasticity* to a certain point. The brain can, in fact, grow new cells and make new connections throughout its life. No matter what, it's never okay to willfully subject a child to high levels of conflict. But if this is not entirely under your control, not everything is lost. With support and a safe setting, the brain can heal to some degree and in some ways.

The potential impacts of your separation on your children will depend on how antagonistic it is. As the advice from the co-parents in chapter 5 shows, families that are able to prioritize their children and create parenting magic through lots of hard work see the children thrive. I appreciate that conflict is not always a mutual choice, but more often than not, it is within the power and control of parents to create circumstances in which their children can do well.

Types of Conflict

There are two types of conflict: constructive and destructive. Constructive conflict is conflict, to be fair. But the key to constructive conflict is what the children experience and take in: they witness calm discussion and problem-solving that leads to a resolution.

Destructive conflict is an entirely different animal. Many of us are well-acquainted with it, even those with the most Disneyesque of upbringings. With this type of conflict, kids witness verbal hostility, the silent treatment, intense criticism of one parent by the other, and increasing awareness that they (the kids) are the focus of all the hostility. Over time, this invokes negative responses in the kids.

Conflict becomes damaging when it is frequent, unresolved, and predominately about the children. The children cannot understand why they are the subject of so much stress and conflict, and over time they internalize it and blame themselves for all their adverse childhood experiences, when it has never been their fault.

The ultimate and most terrifying impact of high-conflict situations on children is that they undermine the children's capacity to regulate their own negative feelings of anger, sadness, and fear. It is our job as parents to provide our children with the tools they require to make it through all the situations life will present to them, by showing them how to solve problems, not how to perpetuate conflict.

Impacts on Kids

Parents always want to know what will happen to their kids if they choose X over Y. We seem to need to know the worst before making a decision — as if any bad outcome would be okay. Still, I can understand the natural inclination to gather as much information as possible. It's why I share anecdotal advice from doctors and social workers and psychologists.

Dr. Clinton lays out the impacts of toxic stress on kids by age group in a way that is accessible, straightforward, and helpful. She also makes clear that no age, demographic, gender, or household is immune to poor outcomes. If those who know better do better, then I hope you take all of this to heart.

BABIES

Dr. Clinton says that babies under chronic stress exhibit a number of warning signs. They may appear apathetic and lose interest in their surroundings. A parent or caregiver, for example, may not be able to elicit a smile from them. They can have poor feeding habits or, alternatively, an insatiable appetite. They can often present with the old-school "failure to thrive," where they do not gain weight despite eating. They can have symptoms like vomiting and skin rashes without an associated diagnosis or illness, and they can be generally withdrawn.

CHILDREN

A child responding to toxic stress may daydream excessively or disengage. They may be oppositional or defiant. They may show motor hyperactivity or become accident prone. And, more often, they may present with anxiety, mood swings, impulsive behaviours, and poor sleep patterns.

TEENS

A child of middle-school age or older may present any of the symptoms that a younger child does. But in their case, the stakes for their future are arguably higher, as grades and school performance, friendships, extracurricular activities, and relationships can all be affected.

Tools for Co-Parents

If you are working with your co-parent in a high-conflict situation, even if it feels impossible, like you will never resolve a thing, there are tools you can adapt to your unique circumstances and needs. Dr. Clinton suggests some tried and tested steps to get your difficult or high-conflict co-parent on your side.

EMPATHY, ATTENTION, AND RESPECT

Empathy, attention, and respect (EAR) is an exercise in extreme patience and selflessness. It requires that you, the one who feels the conflict is "happening to you," suppress the urge to attack or criticize the other parent, whose emotional reactivity and distortions are so frustrating. It's difficult, but you can do it.

To connect with your co-parent using EAR you have to *listen*. You'll acknowledge, in basic terms, that your co-parent is upset ("I can see this is upsetting for you"). You'll let them know that you care ("I want to see you do well" or "I want to help" or "I don't like watching you struggle"). Finally, you'll connect with how they must be feeling ("I can understand how frustrated you must be").

A sample EAR statement from Dr. Clinton looks like this: "I can understand your frustration. This is a very important decision in your life. Don't worry, I will pay full attention to your concerns about this issue and any proposals you want to make. I have a lot of respect for your commitment to solving this problem and I look forward to solving it together." It feels so easy when you read it aloud.

Some people will not hear this statement as kind and focused on resolution. They may become angrier because they feel appeased. Be prepared for that, but know that it doesn't always happen. And either way, the technique is worth a try.

Resilience is really just getting from Point A to Point B in a healthy manner. It's the feeling of having been supported and protected through a really trying circumstance or event. You can help your co-parent to feel resilient here. Even if you feel like you don't owe them a goddamn thing. Even if you think you've already done so much or helped more than anyone could. There's still room to do more.

BIFF RESPONSE

You may also choose to communicate by being brief, informative, friendly, and firm (BIFF). Often applied in professional settings, BIFF works when responding to someone who is treating you rudely. It amounts to a quick, civil, but still thoughtful response based only on the facts; it leaves out anecdotal information. For example, when a person tells you emphatically that your toddler in a stroller needs gloves, you smile and say thank you. Keep the commentary on how they should mind their own business to yourself.

Advice for Parents

It may be that you are too spent and unable to get out of your own head to see the impact of your separation or divorce on your children. But it is possible. You can still help them.

As one parent who went through many adverse childhood experiences herself said to me, it is the parent's job to maximize the children's sense of safety, no matter where they are and who they are with. Exposure to stress, especially traumatic or toxic stress, overwhelms a child (really, any person of any age) and undermines their sense of safety and security, so much so that they shift into survival behaviours. A sense of safety is absolutely critical — like protein to muscle — for a child's optimal functioning.

Children will show you that they are upset before they will tell you. That's a general rule. Declining grades, mood changes, dishonesty, disinterest. Or the opposite: separation anxiety, attachment issues, high emotions around transitions. Older kids will lash out in ways that may have bigger consequences, as we know. It can be completely damaging to their futures, their school performance, their friendships and relationships. Everything. Every single thing can be negatively impacted. These are all warning signs.

This is what *can* happen, but I hope you never have to endure it.

Your Mental Health

First let me say, emphatically, that you are probably a parent first. But your mental health matters. It matters.

I could offer all kinds of hollow platitudes: you can't pour from an empty cup; you need to take care of yourself so you can take care of everyone else; self-care; self-love; blah, blah, blah. But these kinds of statements cause more stress. My cup, for example, was almost completely empty, but I was still pouring from it because I didn't have a choice. I felt like even more of a failure when I couldn't support my own needs *and* those of my children, when the truth was the kids were actually doing okay.

Even today, there's still a great deal of stigma about monitoring and supporting your own mental health and that of the people close to you. It's not always easy to find and secure support. It's even harder to find a therapist you connect with (or, let's be honest, that you can afford), or one who understands and is sensitive to any gender, cultural, racial, or religious issues you face.

When, in chapter 2, I tell you to choose a great team, I don't just mean to choose a supportive, solutions-oriented lawyer. I'm also talking about choosing a supportive, highly recommended therapist. There's a reason for this: your lawyer probably makes you feel safe. And you probably feel like confiding in them. But they're not a therapist. And they're probably way more expensive than a therapist.

Choosing a therapist who can guide you through whatever process you adopt for your separation or divorce, even an amicable one, can be invaluable to your ability to successfully move through that process. A therapist will check in on your mental health — something most lawyers are not trained to do — and will provide you with helpful strategies to get you through tougher times.

A great lawyer will tell you to find a good therapist and will even recommend a few to you. It's widely accepted to be an important part of the separation or divorce process. Otherwise, you can find yourself spiralling, being too hurt, sad, or angry to prioritize your kids or to engage meaningfully in discussions about their futures. You may lash out in unexpected ways. It may feel like you're on the outside, watching yourself say and do things you don't want to, but unable to stop yourself. This can trigger feelings of powerlessness.

It's also okay to say you're not ready for things to be over. That doesn't mean the process of separating won't keep rolling along, but it's okay to acknowledge that your life has just had an anvil dropped on it, and you need a minute to shake the stars out of your vision before you stand up and get going.

Mental health work is not linear, either. There will be ups and there will be downs. Sometimes a family law process will feel like a whole lot of downs. Sometimes you'll feel empowered. Sometimes you'll feel neutral. Those feelings are all normal.

Having been through a separation, I truly believe that no matter what brought about the end of the relationship, people grieve, if not for the relationship itself, then for the other losses associated with its end: home, financial security, old neighbourhood, mutual friends, implied Saturday night plans or Sunday brunches.

I very much grieved the loss of the way things were. I craved the normalcy that my marriage had provided and felt completely insecure in the unknown. Those feelings caused me to repeatedly question everything I was doing and how I was doing it, for a long time. Despite knowing in my heart that Steve and I had done all the right things we could, when the separation was actively happening I was not yet ready to accept that everything was changing, that there was going to be a big question mark on my timeline.

I started seeing a great therapist a year or so into my separation and immediately regretted not doing it sooner. I had not prioritized my own mental health the way I should have. I saw the benefit of therapy when I was only a few sessions in, with even very small changes in the way I perceived things and in the way I dealt with them.

I should add that I had considered therapy a luxury — because it is so difficult to access, though it shouldn't be — and it felt like something I didn't deserve. In the beginning I viewed my separation as an obstacle I just needed to buck up and deal with, like a tough file at work or a difficult project at home.

As it turns out, having a person in the background you can tell all your secrets to and who doesn't judge you or necessarily tell you that you've done something wrong is really effective. It's what resilience means: going through a hard time and coming out feeling more than just okay. Feeling supported, carried, and cared for throughout the process.

Mental health is incredibly hard to maintain. There are all sorts of social issues that hinder taking care of your mental health, with social and cultural stigma being the most prevalent. There's the cost, inaccessibility, and lack of availability of support. And then there's you — your biggest critic. You want to do it all and do it right, and you want to emerge okay. A lot of people who have sustained trauma (myself included) are hyper-independent as a response to stress. We've been let down repeatedly by people we love and trust, so we take it all on. And while this is sometimes okay, it's often not. No one has to go through a separation or divorce alone, but everyone has to put the kids — the potential human collateral damage — first. To succeed at taking care of yourself in tandem with putting your kids first, you'll have to work incredibly hard.

> It took me many, many years to get comfortable with the idea of therapy. I mean, I gave clients contact information for therapists that my bosses recommended, I read self-help books, and I talked to people about my problems in an abstract, non-threatening sort of way. But I never felt comfortable with the idea of laying on a couch and talking through things with a stranger.

Now, anyone who has seen a therapist knows that there's rarely a couch involved. I laugh now when I think about that. But when I found my therapist, Olivia, I found a really excellent fit I didn't know could exist between a person seeking help and a helper. At our first session I basically talked and cried and talked some more, for an hour. And she listened. But she also offered validation and tools for future circumstances that might require them and ways to try to deal with things that felt overwhelming.

The most pivotal moment for me occurred when I asked her, after only one session, "So, what's wrong with me, anyway?"

She said, "There's nothing wrong with you. But next time, we're going to talk about what happened to you."

That statement, so simple but so profound, took therapy from being an inaccessible construct to being something that would become infinitely more helpful the more I tried and the harder I worked at it.

11

Putting It into Practice: Making Your Agreement Work

"I always have to be doing something," replied a lovely client I had the pleasure of working with for more than five years on an intensely litigious file. Indeed, I became acquainted with that Type A part of her early on. I remember vividly the day she came into the office to sign a separation agreement. Despite going to court many times, she and her ex finally settled out of court and agreed to enter into a comprehensive separation agreement. Their two kids were grown. She did not work outside of the home. This file had been, for all intents and purposes, her life for the last five years.

Her hand trembled when I passed her my pen to start initialling the bottom right-hand corner of all fifty or so pages. She looked up at me, and through perfect makeup and hair impermeable to wind she said, "Charlotte, what am I going to do when this is done?"

The statement was profoundly sad and jarring. We don't always become fond of clients — often because we see the literal worst of humanity on a semi-regular basis — but I had grown really fond of her. And she was right. What was she going to do now?

This client had spent five years steeped in litigation, in campaigns of ugly letter-writing between lawyers, in huge bills, and she had still arrived at the end of the road with a decent agreement in hand, one that sealed her financial security and brought the finality that had been sorely lacking all these years. Still, it was a weird version of empty-nest syndrome. This baby she'd been nursing — this divorce — was all grown up. She'd need to find a new purpose.

■

What is the worst thing your ex would say about you?

Most of us know without thinking about it too much. Some of us are embarrassed by our answers. Some wish we'd tried harder. Some tried to change but couldn't. Some decided it was for the best to part ways and create a new kind of family.

None of the answers to this question make you a bad person, or a bad parent. You may have been a terrible partner. I wasn't there, and I only ever hear one half of a couple's story. But you can roll up your sleeves and work hard to achieve the best possible outcome for your kids. It will help to know what it could look like if you don't roll up your sleeves. You are not magically protected from an unfavourable outcome.

It's all about hard work.

When Steve and I separated we had two very young kids, including one with several disabilities and a rare disease to boot. Our eldest son, Isaiah, will not likely achieve self-sufficiency or live independently. His care requires an all-hands-on-deck approach, at all times.

You might say that since we are parents to Isaiah, in the truest sense of the word and not the kind who observe their children's lives from the sidelines, then taking pride in how great our children become is a major reason we were able to create the circumstances we enjoy today. And you might even be right.

But the last five years have taught me a lot.

Parenting in my earliest post-separation days was like watching myself from outside my body and being unable to stop the awful words spewing out of my mouth or the big emotional responses rearing their heads. I was sad and I was angry and I was frustrated. And mostly, I was scared shitless.

When I was in high school, my own parents' conflict felt like a scarlet letter. I figured it was obvious to everyone around me that I didn't have a good situation at home. I buried myself in part-time jobs and was always going out, driving my friends places, or staying late at school. I never wanted to be home.

Complicating the situation at home was my much younger sister. I didn't want her to go it alone. Still, at some point I walked away and started to live a life that didn't have yelling in it every single day. It was refreshing, and the impact on my mental health, the lifting of the burden from my nervous system — well, it happened quickly, and I almost immediately felt more at ease.

There are moments post-separation when you start to recognize, in small increments, how okay you actually are. In my case, Steve and I have maintained an air of extreme flexibility so long as it doesn't negatively impact the kids, which is something we monitor on an ongoing basis.

Steve is a basketball referee, and when we were married I often referred to myself as a March widow because of all the time he had to spend away, working at games. Winters were always long and lonelier than the rest of the year because of the basketball season.

In our co-parenting life, we've each had great opportunities come our way that required the support of the other to help with the kids. We still want what is best for each other — even though each other is no longer "us."

One night, Steve was out until just after the kids' bedtime, so instead of interrupting their routine, I went to Steve's house — our old home together — to watch the boys and put them to bed, in the rooms I had decorated when they were babies. I was struck by how much had changed in the house and how much really had not. The artwork we purchased on a family trip to Nashville still hung proudly on the kitchen wall, and the prints we bought on our babymoon to New Orleans were still next to the stove.

Those walls held so many memories. Walking around the house alone while the boys slept, it was hard not to feel big things once again. I looked at a collection of Justin Bieber stickers, circa 2005, that our youngest son had plastered on the fridge door. At the time Steve and I had been so angry, but we laugh about it now. Our family cat was still there to pet, sitting in the same spot on the same couch.

I tiptoed around, waiting for Steve to come home, and felt a weird pang of jealousy. Years back, when we renovated our very old kitchen, I had, in true Charlotte style, screwed up and forgotten to order knobs for the cabinets. We ended up with little crystal pulls that needed industrial-strength clear glue to attach them to every cabinet door, and there were dozens of doors. I'm not handy, but I tried my best to affix those tiny knobs to every door, only to have them systematically start to crack and fall off the doors, or be pulled off by the kids over the next few years. So many knobs were missing, and many times I asked if we could just replace them. And every time, we ended up talking about something else while the cupboard doors hung without knobs and a collection of loose ones amassed in a bowl on the kitchen counter.

That night, I noticed that the knobs had been replaced. All of them. Every last cupboard now had a fully functional, brushed steel-like pull.

All I had to do to get him to replace the knobs, I thought, *was leave*. The new ones weren't my style. And they didn't match the cabinetry at all. But my heart rate didn't increase, and I didn't feel angry. I felt indifferent. Something I would have felt so ridiculously strongly about just a couple of years earlier now elicited, mostly, sympathy for whoever eventually moved in here and had to look at these fugly knobs.

There is no benchmark for how well, or not, you are doing post-separation, but little moments like this let you know you're okay.

I left when Steve got home, much the same routine we'd kept during our marriage — ships passing in the night. I went home relieved that I had much nicer knobs on my cabinets. Grateful for our differences and even more so for our collaboration as parents.

Like I said, I'm no expert, but I feel we're expertly getting through life as a blended family, and that feels like one of the best outcomes for a colossal amount of effort, ever. It's hard sometimes; it's easy other times. Just like life was before any of this.

The Ten Best Tips for Success

Achieving a resolution in your separation or divorce can be hard, even with an amazing team supporting you, but turning those resolutions into real everyday life can be even harder. When you start a new residential schedule for your kids, remind yourselves of the following:

1. Be kind and patient, with yourself and your kids. There's a lot of change, though it's manageable change. Be kind and patient with your co-parent, too — they may experience the transitions differently from you and may be struggling. This is one of your first opportunities to show how supportive of your new co-parent you can be. Looking out for one another might seem weird, but it's important. Their well-being is integral to the kids and to you.

2. Talk about how you feel, ask your ex how they feel, and always check in with your kids about their feelings. Make sure everyone feels supported. Transitions are hard, and it's okay to feel all sorts of things: anxiety, regret, second-guessing — it's all normal.

3. Find things to do that are just for you. Take a class; watch a YouTube tutorial; work through a recipe for some complicated dish your kids would wholeheartedly reject and sit down with nice plates and really enjoy that meal. It's not indulgence — it's those kinds of activities that will make you a *better* parent.

4. Make sure your kids feel loved, but not missed and not essential to your happiness. Your identity as a parent isn't defined by the amount of time you spend with your kids in a given week. You miss them and wish they were with you. Your whole routine is off-kilter. But it's not their job to make you feel better. They're kids.

5. Agree to disagree. This one is really important. A strong parenting plan or separation agreement provides you with a plan of what to do in the event of a major dispute. So try your best to let the little disagreements iron themselves out when they pop up, as they invariably will. Look the other way when one home serves refined sugars and the other doesn't.

6. Be flexible. Leave room for life to happen — snowstorms; traffic; special opportunities to travel; a family wedding on a weekend that doesn't match your residential schedule; kids

who are with one parent but really, really want to see the other. Listen to your kids, validate their feelings, and facilitate what they're asking for.

7. Trust that your kids are okay in the care of the other parent — the same person, however many years earlier, with whom you embarked on a life with children. Would you have looked over their shoulder every minute of the day, supervising their every move, if you were still together? Not likely. Give your co-parent the same implicit trust you want when the children are with you. This is a hard one, especially when we fall into roles where one parent is the primary caregiver. But letting go is integral to the success of your co-parenting relationship. Remember, you cannot control everything that happens in your children's other home. You will never be able to do that, so stop trying. Like, now.

8. Remember that progress isn't linear. The success of your co-parenting relationship may ebb and flow, especially around tax time when you start talking about money matters. The success of your co-parenting during times of tension will be measured by how well your children move through that time and how unaware they are of the tension.

9. Create a code of conduct, like any professionals engaged in a business relationship. Agree to mutually respect each other, past conduct notwithstanding — we're talking about moving on, not stagnating. Set out your mutual objectives for your business project: healthy, smart, engaged kids. Include each other in the kids' day-to-day lives (freely share information and photos, for example). Remember your initial goal of being a family. Family doesn't have a single narrow definition — you are still very much a family today.

10. Focus on moving forward. Your family is in a new spot now. You have the freedom to creatively approach opportunities to make space for yourself that may never have existed otherwise.

There is, without a doubt, all sorts of healing to do. Let it happen, and it will.

■

You have a solid parenting plan or separation agreement, or both. You know exactly what needs to be done and when and how. Chances are you've been in your new normal for a while and are settling in nicely while accepting all the possibilities and limitations that the new arrangements pose both for you and for your kids.

I'm reluctant to tell you, after all this hard work, that there's more to come. You will be co-parents for a long, long time. You'll be co-parents at soccer games and track meets and recorder recitals. You'll be co-parents at graduations. You'll be co-parents at weddings and in hospital waiting rooms when grandkids arrive. You'll be giving speeches together at big events. You'll stand under chuppahs together and side by side at baptisms. You'll be celebrating all the great things that your kids do, that your great parenting played some role in.

And those are the fun things.

You'll also be co-parents at parent-teacher interviews and at emergency medical appointments and during surprise visits to the emergency room. You'll be co-parents when one of you needs surgery and can't do the heavy lifting while you recover. You'll be co-parents when your own parents die. You might be co-parents when your thirteen-year-old shoplifts a lip balm from Walmart or is verging on academic probation. There is so much work to be done yet. In fact, in many ways, it hasn't really begun, tired as I bet you are feeling right now.

Your parenting plan or separation agreement, no matter how excellent, cannot possibly contemplate every scenario (thanks for the life lesson, Covid). You will have to harness power you didn't know you had to push through complicated times, instances where decisions don't come so easily, and circumstances where you and your co-parent may not agree, or where one of you is hell-bent on things being a certain way: the kids going to a certain school, hosting a b'nai mitzvah at a specific locale, taking a trip that exceeds the number of days you're each able to travel with the kids.

There are endless things to disagree about. And even more things on which you can agree. It's just work, either way. And if you're here, you're no stranger to that.

As I've said, it is so, so important to take care of your own mental health. If a person who will support your mental health is available to you, I think you'll find that talking through things with someone who knows you, knows your strengths and limits, and knows that you're capable of making child-focused decisions will help you feel supported, even when the circumstances you may find yourself in as a parent are anything but supportive.

It's also important to remind yourself who you're doing all this hard work for: your kids. And yourself — don't forget yourself. If the advice from doctors and mental health professionals didn't scare you into avoiding conflict, it can be helpful to remind yourself from time to time that the hard work is worth it because your kids are doing well: they're happy and they have two loving, involved parents.

I fondly remember when I moved past being upset about my relationship ending to being immensely grateful for Steve as my co-parent. It was a few weeks after I moved into my new home with my new partner. My new partner and my older son had been at the dog park, where my son loves to go. On the drive home, in the low sunlight of late October, another car ran a stop sign and T-boned them on our street, just two blocks from our new house. I was at home, making dinner, seven months pregnant amid walls lined with unpacked boxes in a place that still smelled like fresh paint. I heard the sirens before I got the text: *We were in an accident. Please come outside.*

I turned the stovetop off and rushed out the door with my younger son. I waddled-ran to the corner, where my partner's SUV was flipped on its top and the fire department was working to remove my son from a window they'd had to smash in. A scene from a TV show.

A crowd had gathered, and I couldn't believe what I was looking at: the car was completely destroyed, but somehow, magically, my son and my partner were mostly okay. Some superficial injuries and a few cracked vertebrae, but alive.

My first instinct was to call Steve once I knew everyone was okay. He was still the person I called for the kinds of things we fear the most. In minutes he was there, and I was in a complete anxiety-ridden panic. We had not hugged in a very long time, but he didn't hesitate to pull me in and tell me everything was going to be okay. Our son had just been in what, by all accounts, was a terrible accident, and Steve knew inherently how to support me even when he needed support himself.

I can recall many moments of immeasurable gratitude for Steve, but this one stands out. If it's possible to have a platonic knight in shining armour, he is mine. Bound forever by these little people walking around with our DNA, we were going to be okay.

Of course, it isn't always like that. But more often than not it is.

I hail from a high-conflict dynamic with now-divorced parents. I remember how it felt to know, without a doubt, that my parents hated each other's guts, and it ate away at me over the most pivotal years of my development. It really skewed my perceptions of marriage and relationships, and it normalized conflict in a way that would prove terribly detrimental. Unlearning things you carried as fact for your whole life is hard but necessary work.

Nearly every adult who is a child of a high-conflict divorced family will tell you that the impact is far-reaching: they still have the lingering anxiety, disordered eating, trust issues, and so on, that come with the territory. At my own wedding, I had to give the security guard a photo of my dad, who had threatened to show up just to ruin the night for my mom. That I was preoccupied with that possibility when I should have been preoccupied with the rest of my life is regrettable and so negatively impactful.

Co-parenting is a job, and then some. It's a job you probably never wanted, but it's the one you've ended up with. You have the power — even if you don't feel like you do and, sometimes, even if your former spouse is impossible — to make it okay. Better than okay, even. You can make it amazing.

Chase co-parenting the way you would have chased the relationship back in the day. Chase it like the job you wanted so badly and got. Chase it like the good grades you pulled all-nighters for or the marathon you trained an entire year for. Like all good things, it is worth the effort and investment. Like all great things, it will benefit so many more people than just you.

What is the worst thing your ex would say about you?

Think about this question as you navigate your co-parenting life. Think about the mark you want to leave on your kids' lives. Think about the parent you want to be and the support you want to give to your co-parent. Remember that this is hard for both of you. Remember that your kids are just kids.

And now go and kill it at co-parenting.

But don't even ask me about step-parenting. That shit is hard.

When I was twenty, I walked into New Tribe Tattoo in downtown Toronto with a drawing on a piece of paper. It was a butterfly composed of my then-boyfriend's initials. I sat down with a tattoo artist, who looked at it and said, "Are these someone's initials?"

"My boyfriend," I said, eyes aflutter, totally in love.

"Okay, yeah, but I don't do that."

"Why?" My dreams of committing that relationship forever to a patch of skin on my body was quickly dying.

"I only do your kids' names. Your kids will always be your kids. Everyone else? Who knows?"

12

Helpful Links and Information

Parenting Plans

The best resources available to you — whether you're just starting out on a co-parenting journey, or you're thinking about doing so in the future, or you're anywhere along the road to co-parenting — are the long-awaited *Parenting Plan Guide* and *Parenting Plan Template* from the Association of Family and Conciliation Courts (AFCC Ontario). Released in January 2020, the guide takes you through the framework of a parenting plan. You and your lawyer can use the template to begin discussing the terms you wish to apply to your unique co-parenting circumstances. See afccontario.ca/parenting-plan-guide-and-template.

Additional clauses that relate specifically to the Covid-19 pandemic but establish the basis for future pandemics or catastrophes can also be found on the AFCC Ontario website. These clauses effectively create temporary parenting plans while people navigate unusual circumstances. You might find them helpful in many unusual instances in the future. See afccontario.ca/wp-content/uploads/2020/04/Covid-19-Clauses-April -15-2020.pdf.

Court Processes

If I haven't managed to scare you away from court, you can view more information about court processes in Ontario on the Superior Court of Justice website: ontariocourts.ca/scj/family.

Finding a Lawyer

Word of mouth is usually the best way to find a lawyer. Sites like Best Lawyers Canada present lawyers who are recognized "based entirely on peer review." The site states that their methodology "is designed to capture, as accurately as possible, the consensus opinion of leading lawyers about the professional abilities of their colleagues within the same geographical area and legal practice area." See bestlawyers.com/canada.

Collaborative Family Law

For more information on collaborate practice, visit Collaborative Practice Canada (collaborativepracticecanada.ca) or, in Toronto, Collaborative Divorce Toronto (collaborativedivorcetoronto.com). On these sites, you can locate not only collaboratively trained family law practitioners, but also collaboratively trained financial professionals and mental health practitioners.

Finding a Mediator

For more information on mediation in family law matters and finding a mediator, visit Family Mediation Canada: fmc.ca.

Finding a Therapist or Mental Health Practitioner

See chapter 2 for a discussion of the different types of mental health practitioners. I find word of mouth to be a very useful tool here, too, if you are comfortable asking other people.

Psychology Today's website has a therapy directory, a useful tool to locate therapists in your area who focus on specific modalities of mental health support. See psychologytoday.com/ca/therapists.

The Canadian Mental Health Association website has comprehensive links to information about mental health and mental illnesses, ways to find their offices in your area, and options for finding help. See cmha.ca.

Domestic Violence and Intimate Partner Violence

If you are experiencing domestic or intimate partner violence, which can include physical or sexual violence or emotional, spiritual, or financial abuse, please seek assistance in the way you are most comfortable doing so: involve your friends, family, church, employer, family doctor, therapist, or other trusted person.

The Ontario government's website has information for people experiencing domestic or intimate partner violence: ontario.ca/page/domestic-violence.

Child Support

Child support in Canada is federally legislated. Your lawyer or mediator will assist you with calculating the appropriate quantum of support payable each month, as well as the rate at which you and your co-parent will share the children's extraordinary expenses (for example, child care, summer camp, and medical expenses not covered by extended health-care benefits). The Federal Child Support Guidelines can be found on the Government of Canada's Justice Laws website: laws-lois.justice.gc.ca/eng/regulations/sor-97-175.

A useful online calculator can be found on the Government of Canada's Child Support website: justice.gc.ca/eng/fl-df/child-enfant/2017/look-rech.aspx.

The Law and Spousal Support

Several resources related to spousal support are available on the Government of Canada's Family Law website:
- Spousal Support Advisory Guidelines: justice.gc.ca/eng/fl-df/spousal-epoux/ssag-ldfpae.html
- *Steps to Using the Spousal Support Advisory Guidelines* by Lonny Balbi
  - With child support formula: justice.gc.ca/eng/fl-df/spousal-epoux/topic-theme/dir/with-avec.html
  - Without the child support formula: justice.gc.ca/eng/fl-df/spousal-epoux/topic-theme/dir/wo-sans.html

The following resources are available on the Government of Canada's Department of Justice website:
- *Obtaining Reliable and Repeatable SSAG Calculations* by John-Paul Boyd: justice.gc.ca/eng/rp-pr/fl-lf/spousal-epoux/calc

- *Spousal Support Advisory Guidelines: The Revised User's Guide* by Carol Rogerson and Rollie Thomson: justice.gc.ca/eng/rp-pr/fl -lf/spousal-epoux/ug_a1-gu_a1

Dr. Jean Clinton and Research on the Impact of Trauma on the Developing Brain

Learn more about trauma and its impact on children on Dr. Jean Clinton's website: drjeanclinton.com.

Resources for Specific Provinces and Territories

ALBERTA

Finding a Lawyer
- Law Society of Alberta: lawsociety.ab.ca/public/lawyer-referral

The Law
- Alberta Courts: albertacourts.ca/pc/areas-of-law/family
- Alberta Government: open.alberta.ca/publications/f04p5

Collaborative Law
- Collaborative Divorce Alberta Association: collaborativepractice.ca

Accessibility: Legal Aid, Pro Bono Work, and Mediation Resources
- Legal Aid Alberta: legalaid.ab.ca/services/family-law/
- Pro Bono Law Alberta: pbla.ca/get-legal-help/legal-resources
- Alberta: alberta.ca/family-mediation.aspx

Mental Health Supports
- Alberta Health Services: albertahealthservices.ca/amh/amh.aspx

BRITISH COLUMBIA

Finding a Lawyer

- Law Society of BC: lawsociety.bc.ca/working-with-lawyers/finding-a-lawyer

The Law

- Parenting Apart: gov.bc.ca/gov/content/life-events/divorce/family-justice/family-law/parenting-apart
- *JP Boyd on Family Law* (ebook): wiki.clicklaw.bc.ca/index.php/JP_Boyd_on_Family_Law
- JP Boyd on Family Law (blog): bcfamilylawresource.blogspot.com

Collaborative Law

- Collaborative Divorce Vancouver: collaborativedivorcebc.com
- BC Collaborative Roster Society: bccollaborativerostersociety.com

Accessibility: Legal Aid, Pro Bono Work, and Mediation Resources

- Legal Aid BC: family.legalaid.bc.ca/separation-divorce
- Pro Bono Collaborative Family Law Project: bccollaborativerostersociety.com/pro-bono-collaborative-family-law-project
- Access Pro Brono: accessprobono.ca
- Access Pro Brono Virtual Family Mediation Project: accessprobono.ca/program/virtual-family-mediation-project

MANITOBA

Finding a Lawyer

- The Law Society of Manitoba: lawsociety.mb.ca/for-the-public/finding-a-lawyer

The Law

- Manitoba: gov.mb.ca/familylaw

Collaborative Law

- Collaborative Practice Manitoba: collaborativepracticemanitoba.ca

Accessibility: Legal Aid, Pro Bono Work, and Mediation Resources

- Legal Aid Manitoba: legalaid.mb.ca/services/services-we-provide/family
- Manitoba: gov.mb.ca/familylaw/resolution/family-resolution-service.html

Mental Health Supports
- Manitoba: gov.mb.ca/mh/mh

NEW BRUNSWICK

Finding a Lawyer
- Law Society of New Brunswick: lawsociety-barreau.nb.ca/en/public/faq

The Law
- Family Law Information Centre: familylawnb.ca
- Parent Information Program: legal-info-legale.nb.ca/en/pip

Accessibility: Legal Aid, Pro Bono Work, and Mediation Resources
- NB Legal Aid Services Commission: legalaid-aidejuridique-nb.ca /family-law-services/family-legal-aid

NEWFOUNDLAND AND LABRADOR

Finding a Lawyer
- Law Society Newfoundland & Labrador: lsnl.ca/public/finding-a-lawyer/

The Law
- Provincial Court of Newfoundland and Labrador: court.nl.ca/provincial /courts/family/familylaw.html

Accessibility: Legal Aid, Pro Bono Work, and Mediation Resources
- Legal Aid NL: legalaid.nl.ca

Mental Health Supports
- Newfoundland Labrador Canada: gov.nl.ca/hcs/mentalhealth-committee /mentalhealth

NOVA SCOTIA

Finding a Lawyer
- Nova Scotia Barristers' Society: nsbs.org

The Law

- Family Law Nova Scotia, Separation/Divorce: nsfamilylaw.ca /separation-divorce
- Family Law Nova Scotia, Mediation: nsfamilylaw.ca/programs-services /mediation
- Family Law Information Program: nsfamilylaw.ca/programs-services /family-law-information-program
- *Parenting and Support Act*: nslegislature.ca/sites/default/files/legc/statutes /parenting%20and%20support.pdf
- Family Support Regulations: novascotia.ca/just/regulations/regs /psfamsupport.htm (for areas outside of Halifax Regional Municipality and Cape Breton)
- *Matrimonial Property Act*: nslegislature.ca/sites/default/files/legc/statutes /matrimon.htm

Collaborative Law

- Collaborative Family Law Nova Scotia: collaborativefamilylawyers.ca

Accessibility: Legal Aid, Pro Bono Work, and Mediation Resources

- Legal Aid Nova Scotia: nslegalaid.ca/legal-information/family-law

---

NORTHWEST TERRITORIES

Finding a Lawyer

- Law Society of the Northwest Territories: lawsociety.nt.ca/for-the-public

The Law

- *Family Law Act*: justice.gov.nt.ca/en/files/legislation/family-law /family-law.a.pdf
- Government of Northwest Territories, *Family Law in the NWT*: justice.gov.nt.ca/en/files/family-law-guide/Family%20Law%20Guide %20-%20March%202021.pdf

Accessibility: Legal Aid, Pro Bono Work, and Mediation Resources

- Government of Northwest Territories: www.justice.gov.nt.ca/en/legal-aid

Mental Health Supports

- Northwest Territories Health and Social Services Authority: nthssa.ca /en/services/mental-health-resources-and-supports

NUNAVUT

Finding a Lawyer

- Nunavut Courts: nunavutcourts.ca/index.php/how-to/42-nunavut-courts/95-find-a-lawyer

The Law

- CanLII: canlii.org/en/nu/laws/stat/snwt-nu-1997-c-18/latest/snwt-nu-1997-c-18.html

Accessibility: Legal Aid, Pro Bono Work, and Mediation Resources

- Legal Services Board of Nunavut: nulas.ca/en/law-line
- Law Society of Nunavut: lawsociety.nu.ca/en/access-justice-program

Mental Health Supports

- Nunavut Tunngavik: tunngavik.com/initiative_pages/suicide-intervention/there-is-help

ONTARIO

Finding a Lawyer

- Law Society of Ontario: lso.ca/public-resources/finding-a-lawyer-or-paralegal
- Advice and Settlement Counsel Project Toronto: ascfamily.com

The Law

- *Family Law Act*: ontario.ca/laws/statute/90f03
- Family Law Information Centres: ontario.ca/page/family-law-information-centres

Collaborative Law

- Ontario Association of Collaborative Professionals: oacp.co

Guides and Precedent Templates

- Separation Agreement Precedent: stepstojustice.ca/steps/family-law/2-make-separation-agreement
- Parenting Plan Guide and Template: afccontario.ca/parenting-plan-guide-and-template

Accessibility: Legal Aid, Pro Bono Work, and Mediation Resources

- Legal Aid Ontario: legalaid.on.ca/services/family-legal-issues

- Pro Bono Ontario: probonoontario.org
- Toronto Family Mediation Services: mediate393.ca
- Ontario Association for Family Mediation: oafm.on.ca

Mental Health Supports

- Black Mental Health Matters: blackmentalhealthmatters.ca
- Ontario Psychotherapy and Counseling Program Referral Directory: referrals.psychotherapyandcounseling.ca
- The Healing Collective: healingcollective.ca (no-wait-list support available)

PRINCE EDWARD ISLAND

Finding a Lawyer

- Law Society of Prince Edward Island: m.lawsocietypei.ca/find-a-lawyer

The Law

- Prince Edward Island *Family Law Act*: princeedwardisland.ca/sites/default/files/legislation/F-02-1-Family _Law_Act.pdf
- Collaborative Family Law: collaborativedivorce.com/public/lawyer _pei.html

Accessibility: Legal Aid, Pro Bono Work, and Mediation Resources

- Prince Edward Island Canada: princeedwardisland.ca /en/information/justice-and-public-safety/legal-aid
- Prince Edward Island Canada: princeedwardisland.ca/en/information/justice-and-public-safety/child -focused-parenting-plan-mediation
- Families Change: pe.familieschange.ca/en/parents/where-can-we-get -more-help

Mental Health Supports

- Canadian Mental Health Association Prince Edward Island: pei.cmha.ca

---

QUEBEC

Finding a Lawyer

- Barreau du Québec: barreau.qc.ca/en/find-lawyer

The Law

- Justice Québec, Family Law Reform: justice.gouv.qc.ca/en/dossiers/family
- Bar of Montreal, *Family Law Self-Help Guide*: barreaudemontreal.qc.ca /sites/default/files/guideassistancedroitfamille_1_an.pdf
- Éducaloi: educaloi.qc.ca/en (plain-language legal information)

Collaborative Law

- Quebec Collaborative Law Group: quebeccollaborativelaw.ca

Mediation

- Association of Family Mediators of Quebec: mediationquebec.ca

Accessibility: Legal Aid, Pro Bono Work, and Mediation Resources

- Commission des services juridiques: csj.qc.ca/commission-des-services -juridiques
- Family Law Services Provided by Legal Aid Offices: justice.gouv.qc.ca /en/couples-and-families/separation-and-divorce/family-law-services -provided-by-legal-aid-offices

---

SASKATCHEWAN

Finding a Lawyer

- Law Society of Saskatchewan: lawsociety.sk.ca/for-the-public/finding -legal-assistance-saskatchewan

The Law

- Family Law: sasklawcourts.ca/queens-bench/family-law
- *Children's Law Act*: canlii.org/en/sk/laws/stat/ss-2020-c-2/latest/ss-2020 -c-2.html

Collaborative Law

- Collaborative Professionals of Saskatchewan: collabsask.com

Mediation

- Saskatchewan: saskatchewan.ca/residents/births-deaths-marriages-and -divorces/separation-or-divorce/early-family-dispute-resolution

Accessibility: Legal Aid, Pro Bono Work, and Mediation Resources

- Legal Aid Saskatchewan: legalaid.sk.ca
- Famli: familylaw.plea.org/resources
- Mediate: mediate.com

Mental Health Supports

- Saskatchewan: saskatchewan.ca/residents/health/accessing-health-care
-services/mental-health-and-addictions-support-services/mental-health
-support/mental-health-services

YUKON

Finding a Lawyer

- Yukon: yukon.ca/en/find-yukon-family-lawyer

The Law

- CanLII: canlii.org/en/yk/laws/stat/rsy-2002-c-31/latest/rsy-2002-c
-31.html
- Yukon Public Legal Education Association, *Splitting Up: The Yukon Law on Separation:* yplea.com/wp-content/uploads/2020/07/Splitting-Up.pdf

Accessibility: Legal Aid, Pro Bono Work, and Mediation Resources

- Canadian Judicial Council, *Family Law Handbook*: cjc-ccm.ca
/sites/default/files/documents/2021/Family%20Handbook%20-%20
ENGLISH%20MASTER%20FINAL%202021-03-30.pdf

Mental Health Supports

- Canadian Mental Health Association Yukon: yukon.cmha.ca

Index

About the Author

CHARLOTTE SCHWARTZ IS A SENIOR family law clerk and parent of four in a blended family. Her own childhood, her background in family law, and her own separation and divorce have served as massive influences in her writing and in her life. Her writing has appeared in *Today's Parent*, *Chatelaine*, the *Huffington Post Canada*, and She Does the City, among others. A part-time, mature English undergraduate student at the University of Toronto, Charlotte was born and raised in Toronto in the Weston neighbourhood and now calls the East End home, where she lives with her four kids, partner, and far too many pets, all within a convenient, twenty-minute walk from her ex-husband's home.